Adolescence and Developmental Breakdown

ADOLESCENCE AND DEVELOPMENTAL BREAKDOWN

A Psychoanalytic View

MOSES LAUFER AND M. EGLÉ LAUFER

Yale University Press
New Haven and London

Published with assistance from the Louis Stern Memorial Fund.

Designed by Nancy Ovedovitz and set in VIP Baskerville type by Eastern Graphics. Printed in the United States of America by Murray Printing Company, Westford, Massachusetts.

Library of Congress Cataloging in Publication Data

Laufer, Moses.
    Adolescence and developmental breakdown.
    Bibliography: p.
    Includes index.
    1. Adolescent psychopathology. 2. Adolescent psychology. 3. Sex (Psychology) I. Laufer, M. Eglé, 1925–   . II. Title. [DNLM: 1. Mental disorders—In adolescence. 2. Psychoanalytic interpretation. 3. Body image—In adolescence. 4. Sex maturation—In adolescence. WS 463 L373a]
RJ503.L37 1984   616.89'17   84-5100
ISBN 0–300–03194–7 (cloth; alk. paper)
ISBN 0–300–03926–3 (paperback)

The paper in this book meets the guidelines for permanence and durability of the Committee on Production Guidelines for Book Longevity of the Council on Library Resources.

10 9 8 7 6 5 4 3 2

TO ANNA FREUD

Anna Freud told us of her pleasure in having this book dedicated to her, but she died before its publication. She was of great help to us over many years in enabling our work to be carried out. Our wish to dedicate the book to her was and is our expression of our lasting gratitude.

Contents

Preface

This book sets out to apply psychoanalytic discoveries to the understanding of the disorders of adolescence, and to their assessment and treatment. Our experience in treating both adolescents and adults has convinced us that the period of adolescence has a specific and essential contribution to make to psychological life and that the psychic disruptions of this period need to be understood differently from those of childhood and adulthood. This difference rests on the fact that adolescence begins with physical sexual maturity, an event which alters the course of psychic development and gives a meaning to psychopathology during this period that is not similar dynamically to psychopathology in childhood or adulthood.

Some years ago, a very simple fact impressed us, one that led us to question some of the existing explanations of the developmental function of adolescence and the meaning of pathology during this period. It seemed that the reported incidence of suicide and attempted suicide was disproportionately high during adolescence and that the conscious decision to kill oneself did not exist as a social or clinical problem before adolescence. Later we realized that our adolescent patients, unlike most of our adult patients, seemed especially vulnerable either to attacking their bodies physically or to doing something that would, in fantasy, alter the image of their bodies, through anorexia, obesity, self-mutilation, or drug-taking and addiction. In addition, every one of our adolescent patients was deeply concerned about the normality or the abnormality of his behavior and thoughts, a preoccupation which invariably referred to sexual normality or abnormality.[1]

From these observations, and from our shared experience in working at an adolescent walk-in service and at a psychoanalytic research center for adolescents,[2] we realized that the same questions could be asked about many adolescents: Why the sudden signs of mental illness, which are readily diagnosed as schizophrenia? Why severe depression, or anorexia, or signs of sexual abnormality, or violence that seems to be not the result of a social norm but a response to inner voices or to the need to keep out of consciousness the feeling of being abnormal?

We concentrate on an examination of the developmental function of adolescence and its relation to the disorders of this period. The view elaborated in this book is that the break in the developmental process of adolescence is the pathology, because the outcome of such a break must be a distorted relationship to oneself as a sexual being, a passive relationship to the parent of the same sex, and the giving up of the wish or the ability to leave infantile sexuality behind. What we think differentiates one form of pathology from another in adolescence is the underlying fantasy that is being lived out and gratified, the extent and the quality of the regression that is interwoven into the specific pathology, and the fantasied nature of the link to the incestuous parent. For these reasons we have not discussed the specific manifestations of psychopathology commonly associated with adolescence.

Nor have we set out to discuss or explain the factors in the person's earlier development that may have caused the psycho-

1. When "he" or "him" is used in the text, the pronoun refers to both male and female adolescents. When we refer specificially to the male, we describe the "boy" and the "male adolescent"; when we refer specifically to the female, we describe the "girl" or the "female adolescent." To ensure confidentiality, all names used in the text are pseudonyms.

2. The Brent Consultation Centre, a walk-in community service for adolescents, makes available help to people between the ages of sixteen and twenty-three. This includes assessment, short-term consultation, and psychotherapy. The Centre for Research into Adolescent Breakdown investigates psychological breakdown in adolescence through psychoanalytic treatment. Such treatment is available to selected adolescents up to the age of nineteen.

pathology in adolescence. Although there is still a great deal of
uncertainty about the specific relationship between early dis-
harmony in development and adolescent pathology, the more
important reason for the omission of such explanations is that
we wanted instead to confine ourselves to an examination of
the period of adolescence itself—to its developmental function,
to the meaning of the presence of psychopathology, to the relation between pathology and the sexual body, and to the associated problems of assessment and treatment. Discussion of precursors of adolescent breakdown would have led us away from
the specific clinical observations of our adolescent patients and
would have added a degree of speculation we have chosen to
avoid.

Many psychoanalytic and psychiatric writers have contributed
to our present understanding of the issues involved in work
with the psychologically disturbed or ill adolescent. Nevertheless, a large part of the professional community remains hesitant to treat such adolescents. To some extent, this reluctance,
which we believe to be largely unwarranted, can be understood
as part of the historical caution or uncertainty in applying psychoanalytic and psychiatric views to a period of psychological
development that is characterized by changes of body and
mind of such a magnitude that they might make our work unpredictable at best and dangerous at worst.

The earlier interest in adolescence was overshadowed by
doubts about the appropriateness of treatment during this
period of development. Most writers concentrated on normal development and mainly described the social or cultural contributions to development or pathology. The studies of the
biological changes during adolescence did not themselves
contribute to an understanding of the psychopathologies, but
they did call attention to the enormity of the physical changes
during this period and indirectly to the sexual and aggressive
potential of the adolescent from puberty on.

Even within psychoanalysis itself, the interest in either normality or pathology during adolescence was minimal, especially
if seen in light of the vast psychoanalytic literature that has ac-
cumulated since Freud's early contributions. Freud's main con-

tribution to an understanding of puberty and the period of adolescence is contained in his "Three Essays on the Theory of Sexuality" (1905), a work that remains fundamental to any understanding of normality or pathology. In addition, the contributions of writers such as G. Stanley Hall, August Aichhorn, Siegfried Bernfeld, Helene Deutsch, Edith Jacobson, Erik Erikson, and Peter Blos have been of essential importance in defining and understanding the vicissitudes of this period and in delineating some of the areas of vulnerability in development in childhood and adolescence.

Along with such major contributions to theory an interest in the treatment of the adolescent developed at the same time. Over the years, the overriding belief was that the traditional treatment which was applied to the adult was not applicable in the same way to the adolescent. A great deal of interest was concentrated on the application of the various therapies to the adolescent—family therapy, group therapy, role-play therapy, counseling, drug therapy—with the assumption that treatment and its success was tied to the suitability of one or another form of treatment. But it also became clear to those who worked with ill adolescents that a serious gap existed in understanding the psychopathologies of adolescence, a problem which remained separate and distinct from the issue of the suitability of a particular treatment.

The assumption that the psychopathologies of adolescence need to be understood from a different starting point than the psychopathologies of adulthood has been of special relevance to us when we consider the psychoses or so-called psychoses that we see in some of our adolescent patients. In the past, we were hesitant about undertaking the psychoanalytic treatment of adolescents showing such manifestations. But we kept experiencing, either in assessment or during the treatment of some adolescents, the feeling that in many instances adolescents were showing signs of what might be considered in the adult to be psychotic but instead were signs of a temporary, although severe, break with reality rather than the presence of an established and irreversible psychotic illness.

Such a possibility would have critical consequences, especially if our assumption that development during adolescence makes a major contribution to adult normality or abnormality is correct. In other words, not to undertake the treatment of an ill adolescent because of manifestations of psychotic functioning or of assumed psychosis, which in assessment might be described or understood as the early signs of the schizophrenias of adulthood, could lose a chance of reversing such severe pathology or, in less favorable circumstances, might at least enable the adolescent to keep a link with his internal and external reality without reaching the point of having to give up that link completely.

Our assumptions about the nature of the conflict which we observe in the adolescent pathologies have helped us formulate some ideas about the vulnerability to a "break with reality," something that seems to increase markedly at puberty itself and later during adolescence. As yet, we do not know how to differentiate accurately between what we refer to as developmental breakdown (which may include a temporary break with reality) and the more organized psychoses such as schizophrenia or depressive psychosis. But it is becoming clearer to us, from our psychoanalytic investigations, that the assessment of a break with reality during adolescence need not be a sign of psychosis or of the early development to psychosis. Instead it may be understood as part of the adolescent's reaction to being overwhelmed by fantasies containing both sexual and aggressive wishes related to his own body, fantasies which are contrary to the person's idealized body image. The image the adolescent had of himself before puberty may have contained the unconscious fantasy of having a body different from the one he knew he had in reality; and it is only at puberty, when his body has become physically, sexually potent, that his efforts to repudiate what is true (either being male or being female) fails him. He may then have to resort to a break with reality as the only means available to him of maintaining the original distortion of the past. Some of the delusional constructs, the paranoid projections, the violent attacks on the body as seen in suicide attempts and in self-mutilation, the hallucinations of the adolescent, may all be understood as part of such a developmental breakdown—where the adolescent rejects his sexually mature body and perpetuates instead a relationship to a fantasied body different from the one he actually has. In this context the issue of male-female differentiation, and its link with the original oedipal resolution, takes on a crucial meaning, especially in the assessment of severity of disorder at puberty and during adolescence.

Freud's assumption that the presence of psychopathology always means a disturbance in the person's sexual life has important significance when applied to the adolescent. When referring to the person's sexual life, Freud meant the inclusion of a range of areas of the person's life—the level and quality of object relationships, the preoedipal and oedipal identifications and their relation to later sexual orientation, the sublimations which encompass the person's intellectual and creative potential, the specific forms of sexual activity included in one's relation to people of the same or the opposite sex, the response to and means of defense against incestuous strivings. In this sense Freud considered the body and the first relationship to one's own body via the mother to be the foundation of future psychic structure—that is, the body ego as the forerunner of the ego organization. If this is so, we may assume that the relationship to one's own body remains a central relationship throughout one's life, even though the psychic meaning of the body alters drastically from one developmental period to the next. We believe that from puberty to the end of adolescence, that is, to about age twenty-one, this relationship to one's own sexually mature body encompasses one's past history and reactivates conflict and anxiety that repeat solutions of the past but within a new and much more dangerous context. The treatment and the study of adolescents who have shown severe disruptions in their relationship to their bodies, as described throughout this book, have afforded us repeated opportunity to observe those ingredients that seem to us to be integral to developmental breakdown and to the later psychopathologies we observe in many adult patients.

I
ADOLESCENT DEVELOPMENT, PATHOLOGY, AND BREAKDOWN

1
Adolescence and the Final Sexual Organization

In trying to be more precise about the contribution the period of adolescence makes to normal psychological development, we realized that we had to be precise not only about our definition of the structure of the psychopathologies in adolescence but also about how this structure differs from that of the neuroses, perversions, and psychoses of adulthood. Freud's belief that perversion, for example, could not be defined as such until the person's sexual orientation was fixed (1905, 162–72; 1919) made a great deal of sense to us when we applied this view initially to the organization of psychopathology during adolescence and later to the developmental function of adolescence. Although Freud chose perversion as his example, he had in mind the development of the person's sexual orientation and the idea that the main means of gratification normally has a fixed and predictable pattern only by the end of adolescence. But he also considered it essential to show that the disorders in sexual life which are present before the main means of gratification has been established must be viewed and understood differently from those that exist afterward.

In our work with adolescents, our clinical observations repeatedly seemed to confirm this assumption about the timing and course of a pathological outcome in sexual development and orientation. If the main means of gratification normally become fixed only by the end of adolescence, we thought it likely that psychopathology too is fixed at that time. But something specific needed to be added to our existing knowledge of

3

the contribution of puberty and its relation to the developmental function of adolescence to bring us nearer to a precise definition of the characteristics of the pathologies of adolescence —characteristics that would enable us to differentiate these pathologies from those of childhood or adulthood. To be able to do this would have extremely important implications for assessment and treatment in adolescence and would, in addition, be especially relevant to the issues of the prevention and reversibility of severe disorders in adolescence and adulthood.

In "Three Essays on the Theory of Sexuality" Freud (1905) begins his essay on "The Transformations of Puberty" as follows: "With the arrival of puberty, changes set in which are destined to give infantile sexual life its final, normal shape." When describing some of the changes that should take place in puberty—and here he was referring to the subordination of component instincts to the primacy of the genitals—Freud stated: "Just as on any other occasion on which the organism should by rights make new combinations and adjustments leading to complicated mechanisms, here too there are possibilities of pathological disorders if these new arrangements are not carried out. Every pathological disorder of sexual life is rightly to be regarded as an inhibition in development" (pp. 207–8). After summarizing his views about infantile sexual life and the pregenital organization of the child, Freud then refers to the period up to puberty as "an important precursor of the subsequent final sexual organization" (p. 234).

Regarding Freud's reference to the changes that occur with the arrival of puberty, we add the following: Puberty—that is, physical sexual maturity and the accompanying physical ability to procreate—activates a process that continues throughout adolescence. It is a process of experiencing, reorganizing, and integrating one's past psychological development within a new context of physical sexual maturity. The prepubertal wishes and fantasies were safe and acceptable before physical sexual maturity, but these same wishes and fantasies will from puberty onward carry a new incestuous meaning. Past normality or pathology will now be experienced and reacted to as signs of sexual normality or pathology. The body, which until puberty was experienced as a passive carrier of needs and wishes, now becomes the active force in sexual and aggressive fantasy and behavior.

Stated in somewhat general terms, our thesis is this: Although the resolution of the oedipal conflict means that the main sexual identifications become fixed and the core of the body image established, it is only during adolescence that the content of the sexual wishes and the oedipal identifications become integrated into an irreversible sexual identity. During adolescence, oedipal wishes are tested within the context of the person's having physically mature genitals, and a compromise solution is found between what is wished for and what can be allowed. This compromise solution, within the variations of normality, defines the person's sexual identity.

We therefore see the main developmental function of adolescence as the establishment of the final sexual organization—an organization which, from the point of view of the body representation, must now include the physically mature genitals. The various developmental tasks of adolescence—change in relationship to the oedipal objects, change in relationship to one's contemporaries, and change in attitude toward one's own body—should be subsumed under this main developmental function rather than viewed as separate tasks. The manner in which the adolescent deals with these developmental tasks enables us to know whether there is a continued progressive move to adulthood or whether therapeutic intervention is necessary. Once this final sexual organization is established, there no longer is a choice for any kind of internal compromise, such as may have existed earlier in adolescence. What we then see in young adults, at least in their pathological disorders, is the result of a breakdown in the developmental process that took place in adolescence.

Later in this chapter we shall present clinical material from the analyses of a late adolescent and a young adult to clarify the nature of these new arrangements in adolescence and of the pathological disorders in young adulthood that reflect the breakdown of the developmental process during adolescence. We show how these new arrangements are tied to the manner in which the content of the central masturbation fantasy is integrated into the person's final sexual organization by the end of adolescence and how this reflects the way in which the adolescent has, by the end of this developmental period, integrated the physically mature genitals as part of the representation of the body.

THE CENTRAL MASTURBATION FANTASY

We assume that, as part of normal development from infancy, a person finds means of gratifying instinctual demands by using either his own body or an object (Freud 1905; Mahler 1974; Schilder 1935). The preoedipal child may have available a whole range of autoerotic activities, games, and fantasies that help to recreate and relive the relationship to the gratifying mother. After the resolution of the oedipus complex and the internalization of the superego, however, we can no longer refer in the same way to the child's means of gratifying his instinctual wishes and demands in relation to his first love object, the mother. With the resolution of the oedipus complex, all regressive satisfactions will be judged by the superego as being either acceptable or not. Moreover, in terms of the future sexual orientation and the final sexual organization of the person, the resolution of the oedipus complex fixes the central masturbation fantasy—the fantasy that contains the various regressive satisfactions and the main sexual identifications. The fate of this fantasy is of special significance in understanding normal and psychopathological development in adolescence, and the way this fantasy forms part of or interferes with development during adolescence can be seen later in the person's adult life.

This central masturbation fantasy is, we believe, a universal phenomenon and itself has nothing to do with pathology. During childhood and latency its content remains unconscious but is expressed in a disguised form via daydreams, or fantasies that accompany masturbation, or games or make-believe activities and relationships (A. Freud 1965). Although the reactions of the latency child and the preadolescent to this fantasy and to various forms of autoerotic activity are determined mainly by the reaction of the superego, with the physical maturation of the genitals the content of the fantasy takes on new meaning and makes demands on the ego that differ qualitatively from the earlier ones. Although the content of the central masturbation fantasy does not normally alter during adolescence, the fact that it is experienced within the context of having physically mature genitals means that the defensive organization is under much greater stress.

We have found that, after puberty, a compelling quality may be added to this fantasy, with the need for it to be lived out in object relationships and in one's sexual life and with the feeling that the only gratification that really matters is the one that also represents unconsciously the living out of that fantasy. The compelling quality is frightening to the adolescent because of the power and destructiveness that may then be added to the fantasy and because of the ease with which reality may be denied at the time the fantasy is being lived out. This fantasy becomes an integral part of the patient's experience of the transference and is often secretly the basis of the gratifications obtained from treatment. It is our impression that much of the acting-out behavior that we associate with adolescence and often accept as part of normal development reflects the adolescent's efforts to find new ways of integrating the central masturbation fantasy. Similarly, some of the breakdowns or temporary psychotic episodes that manifest themselves in adolescence represent the only solution available to the ego (even though it is a pathological solution) in the effort to find new ways of integrating the content of the central masturbation fantasy within the context of genitality. The clinical material illustrates some of these points.

We want to avoid the impression either that these core fantasies are readily available to consciousness or that the analyst's main function is to put together the core fantasies while disregarding the rest of the person's functioning. Of course this is not so. It will undoubtedly take a long time to construct in one's own mind a patient's central masturbation fantasy, but the clues are there in the clinical material, in the whole range of derivatives from the unconscious—such as repeated daydreams, object relationships that take on meaning for the patient, the fantasies that accompany the patient's masturbation or other sexual activities, and repetitive forms of behavior that may be understood partially as an undoing of the repression. In our work with the ill adolescent, these entries into the unconscious enable us, over a period of time, to put together the fantasy, which then permits us to understand the motivation, the power of certain kinds of gratifications, and ultimately the pathology. These fantasies will not themselves tell us about the history of their development, nor will piecing them together assure anything but an insight into the unconscious and a meaning of the pathology. The history of the development of these fantasies can only be gained through understanding them within the context of the transference. But to establish what is the core fantasy is a necessary part of the treatment and of the undoing of the illness.

The presence or the significance of the central masturbation fantasy is in no way dependent on whether the person masturbates or not. Instead, it is important to keep the link, at least in our understanding of the patient's pathology, between his present sexual life and object relationships and his infantile sexuality—which means his autoerotism, his early relationship to the gratifying object, his preoedipal fantasies and relation to reality, and the changing relationship to his own body as a source of gratification. In our experience, it is not at all uncommon for the adolescent patient (or the adult) to have found ways of completely repressing any memory of early autoerotic activity and to present himself as someone who has few, if any, fantasies and who may even have given up the conscious wish for any sexually gratifying relationships in his present life. But such an outcome is part of the patient's pathology and in no way diminishes the presence or the power or the status of this fantasy; it only means that it may be a much more delicate task to unearth the fantasies and to establish their meaning in the life of the patient.

LATE ADOLESCENCE AND YOUNG ADULTHOOD

Through trial action, the adolescent will seek a compromise answer that, optimally, enables him to satisfy the wishes contained in his central masturbation fantasy, while at the same time obtaining superego approval by satisfying the demands of conscience and the expectations of his ego ideal. This means that, normally, the adolescent must have available some age-appropriate ways of finding gratification and new objects. Having physically mature genitals means that regressive wishes can no longer be allowed the same freedom as before because now those wishes may threaten the defense organization and bring about superego condemnation. The problem can be considered a developmental one when genitality remains the main means of gratification. As is often the case in pathological development, however, we see severe interference in the adolescent's ability to use masturbation and the accompanying fantasies as trial action if the pregenital wishes override genitality. This is especially so in late adolescence, from about the age of sixteen. Instead, the sexually mature body is experienced as the source of these regressive wishes, resulting in the need to repudiate it as the means through which gratification can be obtained (Blos 1972; Ritvo 1971). Because of the wishes contained in the central masturbation fantasy, the adolescent may feel in constant danger of giving in to what he both wants and must not allow. In the face of these demands, he feels passive or, perhaps more correctly, helpless. As a result, he may renounce his ability to control his body or the sensations coming from it.

The process is different in normal development during this period. However much the adolescent feels in danger of giving in to regressive wishes, he still has the unconscious awareness that a choice exists. If we examine the direction of the libido and the relationships to objects as expressed in the fantasies and especially in the masturbation fantasies, we find that the libido is object-directed, even though the gratification is of a narcissistic or autoerotic nature. At the same time, the masturbation fantasies of adolescents who are developing normally, especially older adolescents, include the active seeking of a sexual love object. Normal progressive development and the "trial action" solutions during adolescence have an active quality—that is, the adolescent feels that he is at least partially in charge and in control—whether he imagines himself the active or the passive one in the fantasy. The important factor from a developmental point of view is the feeling that he still has *the choice to be active or passive within the sexual role*. This factor defines the nature of progressive development in adolescence and conveys that the final sexual organization is in the process of being established. It implies that genital as well as pregenital wishes contained in the central masturbation fantasy can still be used actively in the attempt to find an answer. While this may be a compromise answer, nevertheless, genitality is the final victor.

Something different happens in the adolescents whose defense organization is incapable of warding off the regressive pull of pregenital wishes (Deutsch 1932; Harley 1961) and who experience the living out of the central masturbation fantasy mainly as being repetitively overwhelmed. They then experience their sexual body as the source as well as the representative of their abnormality. For these adolescents, the predominant wishes remain pregenital, thus precluding the use of masturbation as a trial action; instead, sexual gratification from their bodies acts as a constant proof that they have surrendered. In these adolescents, the final sexual organization may be established prematurely—either because the choices are nonexistent or because they view choice as an additional threat to an already precarious defense against further regression.[1] What we see then, especially in older adolescents and young adults, is the pathological answer to the conflict that existed during adolescence; it is as if they have accepted that genitality, with regard to both object relationships and gratification, either cannot or must not be attained. They have accepted the fact that there no longer is a choice.

CLINICAL MATERIAL

The clinical material is taken from the analyses of two male patients, an adolescent and a young adult. Although this material

1. See chapters 10 and 12.

may seem to represent the extreme of what we meet in analytic work, it highlights the main points of this chapter: the part played by the central masturbation fantasy in the establishment of a final sexual organization by the end of adolescence, and the difference in development and functioning between the adolescent and the young adult.

The Adolescent Patient: Mark

Mark was in analytic treatment for four and a half years, from the age of sixteen and a half to twenty-one. Although he first sought help for migraine, depression, and poor attendance at school, it was really his behavior during masturbation that worried him, conveying to him that he was either mad or perverted. Most often he masturbated in the nude. He liked to have his anus exposed and his buttocks very tensed. Sometimes he hit himself on his back. At other times he crawled about on the floor growling, with the pleasurable idea that somebody might enter his anus; or he masturbated in the living room while his mother was ostensibly asleep in one of the armchairs, placing himself either behind or beside her.

Except for the sudden tragic death of his father when Mark was twelve years old, his history before adolescence sounded uneventful and not unusual. But it soon became obvious that some of his relationships during latency, especially his relationship to the church, foreshadowed the pathological development that became obvious during adolescence. When he was alone in the church, he would walk around it with a huge load of books on his back until he was utterly exhausted—a behavior in which he lived out part of his central masturbation fantasy. The savior theme and its relation to his masochism and his need to be humiliated played a very important part in his adolescence.

After Mark had been in treatment for nearly two years, his previously casual drug taking developed into an addiction to methedrine; soon thereafter he stopped coming to treatment. During this time, he was near death. Although we will not discuss some of the technical problems encountered, it was an error by the analyst to allow Mark to give in to the fantasy of being castrated, helpless, a girl. It was obvious throughout his treatment that his castration wish was much greater than his castration fear; the treatment, and later the drug addiction, meant for Mark giving in to his feminine wish and perpetuating the central fantasy of being loved, humiliated, and saved.

We have come across this wish in the treatment of other male adolescents, but the fear of castration and the identification with the oedipal father enable some of them to give up the wish to submit passively to the father and to repress or integrate the derivatives of this passive wish. This process, which can be considered part of normal adolescence, was missing in Mark because his actions, masturbatory as well as others, were always tied to the central masturbation fantasy. None of the regressive behavior and fantasies was ever separated from this fantasy or subordinated to genitality.

He described how, a year or so before he came to treatment, he had dressed up in his mother's slip, pretending that he was a girl. The dressing up was always accompanied by masturbation. His concern about his body, and the need for him or his mother to do things to it, had persisted for a long time. As a child he had worms, and his mother would regularly clean his anus. He sometimes thought that the worms had something to do with having been or becoming a girl. The link with a pregnancy fantasy is clear, but it is of interest that when such an interpretation was made it had no effect whatsoever on him. He recalled having been told by his parents that, had he been a girl, he would have been named after his father's favorite sister, and he believed that if he had been a girl he would have been loved more by his father. But to be loved by the father also seemed to contain Mark's wish to be humiliated and punished. Being a girl, having his body cared for, and being humiliated were woven into his masturbation fantasy and were in fact the dominant themes. In the fantasy he was identified with the woman who was being penetrated by the big, powerful man. The feeling of helplessness following masturbation offered him a great deal of satisfaction; he felt cared for and temporarily at one with his mother.

During the last year of treatment it was possible to detect a significant change in his masturbation fantasy. Mark began to find it pleasurable to think of having intercourse with one of the girls he knew at his college. The analyst's concern was that, within the transference, this was another capitulation by Mark, but gradually he began to test this fantasy in his real relationships. He started to date girls and, after having been out with a girl, was able to masturbate with the thought of penetrating her.

To understand what had happened, it is necessary to go back to the period just prior to the time he became addicted to methedrine, when he was eighteen. His mother had become ill with diabetes. Mark began to stay away from school and spent many hours lying on the floor. Even though he was temporarily elated when his mother began to get better, his anxiety about her health and his fear that she might die played an important part in his feeling of hopelessness and in his wish to give in and die. He left his school, took a night job, and spent the day high on drugs. He described his feeling after injecting himself with methedrine as "lovely, the penis shrinks, and it's almost impossible to get an erection—but it doesn't matter, because at times like that you don't need a penis." Soon after he left school, he stopped coming to treatment. He stayed away for a month and returned only after the analyst telephoned and said he wanted him to return. Some time later he could tell the analyst how, while he was lying in his room with syringes by his side, his mother would come in, talk with him, and behave as if nothing was happening. (The analyst could not establish whether this was mainly fact or fantasy.) He would then feel as if nothing mattered, as if nobody cared, so he might as well die. He could also tell the analyst that during the time he was injecting himself, and when he was deciding to leave school, he had secretly hoped that the analyst would do something to show that he cared for him. When the analyst did not, Mark felt he might as well give in because nobody was helping him to live. This feeling also contained elements of his relationship to his dead father—as if his father and now the analyst had withdrawn from him and were forcing him to become a girl.

He was saying that he needed somebody to enable him to respond to the internalized conflict. He could not do it alone partly because the giving in, the dying, and the waiting to be saved were such integral parts of his central masturbation fantasy. He was waiting for either his mother or the analyst to take over his body and help him, but when his mother and the analyst behaved as if they did not want his body, he thought there was no way out of his deadlock.

During the second part of the treatment, various crises arose with which the analyst was able, technically, to deal quite differently than he had in the past. Mark wondered about drugs, and he thought of attacking the analyst in some way by again breaking down. Yet he also began to have different masturbation fantasies, some of which included the analyst. In one version, he would suck the analyst's penis and feel loved by him. In another, people were rolled up into small balls—a representation of complete withdrawal, of the wish to suck his own penis, to be totally self-sufficient—in other words, to be both male and female.

It is clear that Mark's breakdown was equivalent to giving in because of his feeling of hopelessness and his belief that the people who now mattered most, his mother and the analyst, did not care. The analyst was finally able to help him because the process of treatment enabled him not to surrender completely to the pull of the wishes contained in his central masturbation fantasy. The analyst's response to him, as well as his mother's great concern for him when she improved from the diabetes, helped to create a deadlock—that is, it kept the conflict alive. Treatment did for Mark what happens normally during the latter part of adolescence: It let the identification with the oedipal father come to the forefront and helped him to use it in establishing his final sexual organization. Without treatment, the deadlock would have resulted in a giving in; that is, by the end of adolescence his passive wishes to give in, to be a girl and to have his mother do with his body what she wished, would have become integrated into the image of himself. His future is still precarious, but without treatment during adolescence, *before* the establishment of a final sexual organization, the outcome in young adulthood would have been one of perverse sexuality,

few if any relationships to people, and possibly a giving in to
the point of deciding to die.

The Young Adult Patient: Paul

Paul was in analytic treatment for just over one year, at the age
of twenty-three. He did not return to treatment following a
summer break, saying that he had had enough of "being
forced" to change by his mother and the analyst and that he
would henceforth organize his life on his own. For Paul, treatment and change meant that he would lose his only means of
sexual gratification. He left treatment at the point when he experienced the analyst as the mother who would take away this
secret gratification.

He was referred after he had been asked to leave a psychiatric hospital because he would not accept the hospital rules in
general but mainly because he continued to bring drugs into
the ward. The analyst's knowledge of Paul's history before adolescence was limited. Paul remembered his childhood as a time
when everything he did revolved around his mother—playing
in the garden, going places with her, and waiting for her to
have time for him so that they might go for walks or shopping.
At the age of seven he went to a boarding school some distance
from home. Although he was very unhappy for a time, he "got
used to it." He made some friends, but most of the time he
spent alone. The picture he had of that period was of being
teased and bullied, crying in his room, waiting for his parents
to visit, and dreading the time when the visit would end.

At the age of eighteen, still at the boarding school, he attempted suicide and was admitted to the local mental hospital,
where he stayed for some months. The suicide attempt was not
taken seriously by either his family or himself. He went on to a
university where, after a few weeks, he made another suicide
attempt and then left the university. He did nothing for some
months, but during this time he began to smoke a great deal of
marijuana, which he continued to do throughout the period of
treatment.

At the boarding school he had begun to feel that something
was wrong with his thoughts. The only thing that could com-

fort him during his periods of despair and emptiness was his teddy bear, which he had had since early childhood. He still had it, and it remained important to him. At the school and later he would hug it close to him, and this would help to remove the empty hole he felt existed inside his chest. At school he had begun to feel that anything was better than having nobody to love him, and he still believed that it was this that made him think that a homosexual relationship was at least a way of being held and cared for.

He had a close relationship with one boy of his own age; they masturbated each other, and Paul let his anus be investigated, "but that was all." He recalled it as something he did not like much, "but it was better than crying." Following the suicide attempt and after leaving the university, he met a man a few years older than himself with whom he had a homosexual relationship. This included fellatio, anal intercourse, and Paul's being tied to a bed after which the man masturbated him. Paul said he did not mind this because at least somebody was interested in him.

During the period of the treatment, and for some time prior to it, he had almost no contact with his parents. He believed that all they wanted was to get him to conform and to be a good son. He repeatedly stated that he did not care what happened to either parent, but at the same time he waited anxiously for letters from his mother.

For much of the year in treatment, he was unable to keep a job because of the difficulty he had getting up in the morning. He used to go to sleep between 3 a.m. and 7 a.m., having spent most of the night either drinking or smoking hash. He told the analyst that as a child he was terrified of the dark and needed his mother to be with him when he went to bed. When she left the room, he would have to hug his teddy bear; otherwise he was frightened that something might happen to him. At boarding school this was easier to cope with because there were other boys in the room and he could feel safe with them, but he still needed his teddy bear in bed. Now he had to drink each night or smoke hash until he was unaware of where or who he was.

This was the only activity that enabled him to dull the part of his mind that said he was bad or dirty. If he lay in bed at night and was not drunk or high on drugs, part of his mind would attack him and say he was useless and bad. But during the day, he was not aware of this part of his mind, so long as he could feel that his mind and his body were under control—that is, so long as he felt nearly dead most of the day. He spent much of his time either looking for places to buy marijuana, wandering the streets, or visiting people whom he had met at the hospital, who would then feed him and care for him.

His masturbation activity and fantasy had continued without much change since his early adolescence. He would first drink or smoke hash; then he would lie on the floor in the dark imagining somebody doing something to him (he said he could not be sure what). He would then switch on the light and put on his mother's dress. Then he would undress, hit his back or buttocks, and masturbate. He could not be sure who was hitting him. This made him feel good because the alcohol, the masturbation, and the hitting deadened him for the rest of the day. The nearest he got to describing what fantasy was active during the time he was hitting himself was to say that he felt somebody was caring for him. An aunt appeared in the fantasy a few times, but he had no idea what she was doing.

During the period of treatment, it was extremely difficult to reconstruct the time in adolescence when he felt that his world had collapsed and began to believe that nothing could be changed. It was as if the experience of the breakdown—exemplified by his suicide attempt and his admission to the mental hospital—was traumatic inasmuch as he felt completely overwhelmed by internal forces without having any ability at that time to cope with them. Nor did he feel that he could turn to the outside world for help in dealing with these forces. He could only say that this time was lonely and that he did not care whether he lived or not. He wanted to die, he said, when he felt sure that his mad thoughts and his activity during masturbation would never change. Internally, during the time of his breakdown in adolescence and later in treatment, he felt that nothing mattered, that there was nothing he could do about his sexual life or about his relationships to other people, and that if he died it simply was "too bad."

Part of the initial task in treatment was to try to reawaken a feeling of wanting or needing people. For a while he felt that the analyst was the only person he could trust and that only in treatment could he risk showing the extent of his despair. For the first time in years he could talk about and begin to feel the severe depression and the feeling of emptiness underlying his present behavior. But this was something much too painful to experience. He said that he had begun to dread coming to see the analyst, even though Paul liked him, because the analyst talked about things he wanted to forget and that he had begun to believe did not matter any longer. He now thought of the analyst as the person who might make him remember the most terrible time in his life (referring to both the time he went to boarding school and the time in his adolescence when he felt he was becoming a pervert; worst of all was the feeling that no-body cared what happened to him at either time).

When he felt that the analyst cared for him, he was able to find work for a while and could begin to express some annoy-ance with himself for being so dependent on drugs and with the drug pushers who he felt were living off his weakness. He could even begin to feel that he missed the analyst during the holiday breaks. But at the same time he was convinced that the treatment was not really doing anything to help him change his attitude toward his body and particularly to his penis. It was as if the beginnings of longing for people emphasized for him the extent to which he had, from the time of his breakdown in ado-lescence, tried to find ways of excluding any objects from his sexual life. His present sexual life, which consisted mainly of masturbation, lying in bed with his teddy bear, or caressing his body, contained the repetitive living out of his central mastur-bation fantasy and the defense against the anxiety aroused if he felt dependent on anybody. Via the drugs, his teddy bear, and being cared for by various people, he could feel that the image of himself as somebody with a nonfunctioning penis did not matter; instead, to be cared for as he was now perpetuated the idea that he had successfully disowned his sexual body and had given in completely.

From Paul's description of his actions and thoughts during masturbation, it seemed that his final sexual organization had become established at the time of the breakdown in adolescence; very little had changed in his life since that time. There was no change at all in his masturbation fantasies; unaltered, they had become integrated into his character. It was as if his whole life now was a repetitive living out of his central masturbation fantasy. Moreover, he seemed to feel compelled to live his life in a very specific way. The developmental possibilities that may have existed during adolescence were destroyed at the time of the breakdown.

SOME IMPLICATIONS FOR TREATMENT

If it is a psychological fact that a person's final sexual organization is established by the end of adolescence, a correct diagnosis and treatment in adolescence can be important for the whole future life of that person. There are therapists who hold that adolescence is a time when treatment, especially intensive treatment, is contraindicated. The views in this chapter suggest why we think that such a belief is incorrect. If the developmental process in adolescence either is seriously interfered with by internalized conflict or has stopped as the result of a breakdown in functioning, then we say treatment is not only indicated but urgent. It is urgent because we may still be able to aid progressive development and help the adolescent to integrate genital functioning into his final sexual organization. Some adolescents are prone to severe and quick regression and are in danger of organizing their lives, as Paul did, almost totally around the living out of their central masturbation fantasy. As we have tried to show in the clinical material, prognostically the signs for future pathology are serious when a breakdown occurs that halts the developmental process or is experienced as a traumatic episode.

With young adults, additional important items, both diagnostic and therapeutic, need to be considered. Care needs to be taken not to regard behavior or thought which is characteristic of adolescence as a sign either of some transitory interference in development or of "prolonged adolescence" (Bernfeld 1923; Blos 1954). Instead, such behavior indicates that the person was stuck in his development in adolescence—what we now see is the pathological solution of the earlier conflict. At the time of the move from adolescence into young adulthood, around the age of twenty-one, a person's way of dealing with anxiety becomes much more predictable; the quality of his object relationships is set; and the channels for libidinal gratification have become much more specific.

2
Developmental Breakdown

In our clinical work, we were led to the conclusion that manifest disruptions in behavior and functioning during adolescence are preceded by a developmental breakdown at puberty. The consequence of such a disruption is that the developmental function of adolescence—establishing a final sexual identity—is seriously affected. In this chapter we concentrate on aspects of this function which are important to an understanding of developmental breakdown and its relation to later pathology.

Our views about psychopathology in adolescence—its organization, assessment, and treatment—rest on our view of the meaning to the adolescent of a developmental breakdown at puberty. One central assumption in this concept is that there is a definite interrelationship between body-image unification, ultimate male-female differentiation, the resolution of the oedipus complex, and the time when psychopathology becomes established and irreversible—that is, irreversible without therapeutic help. We date this pathological organization as finally taking place by the end of adolescence. This implies, then, that developmental breakdown is a critical occurrence with a cumulative effect throughout adolescence, with serious implications for normality and psychopathology in adulthood.

We have been struck over and over again by the numbers of patients who report that they felt everything was going well, more or less, until something happened suddenly in their adolescent or adult lives, after which things were never the same again. We refer to those patients who come for help with manifestations of pathology such as severe depression, attempted suicide, perversion, psychoticlike functioning with an accompanying flood of compelling fantasy and action, anorexia, and the like. But in every psychoanalytic treatment we have carried out of people with such manifest disturbances, it has been possible to formulate, as well as therapeutically important to reconstruct, that they experienced a *developmental breakdown* at puberty. This breakdown was lived out in some way but at a very heavy price, distorting their object relationships, forcing them to find means of fooling their consciences so as not to feel tormented by their guilt about sexuality or about regressive fantasy, or in some instances deadening their feelings to the point that their relation with the real world was severely hampered, sometimes to the point of presenting psychoticlike features.

In our adolescent patients the breakdown (which had not yet been unified fully into a pathological organization) manifested itself in such behavior as physical attacks on one of the parents, suicide attempts, the compulsion to become involved in activities that endangered their lives or made them feel that their sexuality was no longer a problem, or, at the other end of the spectrum, promiscuity and a range of frantic efforts to change their images of their bodies and the use they made of their bodies with a person of the same or the opposite sex.

THE TIMING OF THE DEVELOPMENTAL BREAKDOWN

We do not view the disorders of adolescence as similar to those of childhood or of adulthood, even though some disorders (for example, anorexia, obesity, and some of the perversions) may share a common fantasy whenever the pathology manifests itself. We define developmental breakdown in adolescence as the unconscious rejection of the sexual body and an accompanying feeling of being passive in the face of demands coming from one's own body, with the result that one's genitals are ignored or disowned or, in the more severe cases, the feeling that they are different from what one wanted them to be. It is a breakdown in the process of integrating the physically mature body image into the representation of oneself.

Whatever the actual disorder, the specific interference in the

developmental process that can be defined as adolescent pathology is contained in the adolescent's distorted view of and relationship to his body, expressed via hatred or shame toward the
sexual body. Unlike the child or the adult patient, the adolescent patient experiences his body as the constant representative
of that which will overwhelm him with painful or frightening
fantasies and emotions. He experiences his body as constant
proof that he has given in or surrendered passively, with the
feeling that he has submitted to regressive demands. Being the
victim of the regressive pull is often expressed by projecting
the hatred of his own body onto the mother, with the feeling
that he has now surrendered to her.

The developmental breakdown takes place at puberty, and
its timing is tied directly to the adolescent's reaction to the sexual maturation of his body.[1] For the male, this maturation
means the ability to produce semen, to ejaculate, and to im-
pregnate the female; for the female, it means ovulation, the
ability to become pregnant and grow a child in her body, and
to menstruate at regular intervals when not pregnant. The
breakdown at puberty expresses the adolescent's anxiety or
panic when he or she suddenly is faced with a sexually mature
body. The severity of the breakdown and its consequences
throughout adolescence and adulthood are determined by the
unconscious meaning the adolescent gives to this sexual body
and the extent to which the defensive organization becomes
disrupted.

The effects of developmental breakdown may become obvious immediately at puberty or only much later in adolescence.
If they become obvious soon after puberty, it is a sign that the
breakdown is related to the direct incestuous wishes of the adolescent or to the anxiety provoked by the destruction of the
fantasy of not being required to choose between having either
a male or a female body. This points to the possibility that the
function of reality testing is now seriously damaged, either
temporarily or permanently. A breakdown at puberty may

1. We think that the developmental breakdown in adolescence has its history
in a developmental breakdown at the time of the oedipal resolution, but up to
now we have not found sufficient clinical evidence to confirm this hypothesis.

manifest itself in a range of ways—withdrawal from contemporaries; secret, compulsive masturbation with accompanying sadistic or perverse actions; sudden attacks on the oedipal parent; school phobia that seems to begin at puberty; denial of pubertal changes and near-conscious efforts to change the pubertal body to a prepubertal one; injury or damage to one's body; and conscious efforts to die or to kill oneself.

Although the breakdowns that become evident only later in adolescence need to be viewed seriously as well, the ability of the adolescent to function without severe disruption for some time after puberty implies that the defensive organization has successfully, even if only temporarily, enabled him to find some displaced answers to his direct incestuous wishes, with a somewhat lesser likelihood of severe damage to the function of reality testing. A later breakdown—as manifested in attempted suicide, anorexia, serious drug taking or addiction, homosexuality, severe depression, sudden academic failure—is more a sign of rejection of the sexual body after an effort has been made at some kind of integration of the physically mature genitals as part of the body representation. The projections of these adolescents may be very disruptive to their day-to-day functioning and may seriously affect their ability to differentiate reality from fantasy, but the damage to the mental structure seems less severe than is the case for those adolescents whose breakdowns are obvious at puberty.

In breakdown the unconscious meanings that the adolescent can give to the significance of his sexually mature body have limited possibilities, even though the range of manifest behavior seems so vast. These include the destruction of oedipal identifications, the possibility of incest, the possibility of developing in a sexually abnormal way, the loss of narcissistic perfection, and the fact of having either a male or a female body even though this may be denied in fantasy.

Whatever meaning any one of these possibilities has for the adolescent at the time of the breakdown, it has a direct link to the adolescent's reaction to having to separate his body from his incestuous objects and his oedipal past and to differentiate it into either a male or a female one. In normal development, the adolescent knows unconsciously that choices still exist for him in his sexual life. This includes the move away from incestuous objects to other relationships—a move that also allows for a choice of those gratifications which will remain dominant throughout later life. But the adolescent who has experienced a developmental breakdown is unconsciously aware that this kind of choice does not exist; instead he feels that the choice or the outcome lies outside himself or is in the power of somebody or something within his body.

MALE-FEMALE DIFFERENTIATION

Although the precursors of male-female differentiation are established during the oedipal period and are tested throughout latency, only by the end of adolescence is the image of oneself as being either male or female finally established. But the outcome is very different in normal development than it is in development that is disrupted by a breakdown.

In normal development the adolescent will find it possible to use relationships, autoerotic activities, fantasies, and various forms of trial action to enable him to establish an image of his own body which includes his own sexually mature genitals and also the recognition and integration of the genitals of the opposite sex. Such a developmental process represents the ability to give up the oedipal incestuous wishes. It means also the ability by the end of adolescence to restore the oedipal parents internally—that is, unconsciously to cease blaming the oedipal parents for earlier failures. The result is an internal freedom to acknowledge that the original oedipal wish and demand contained an unfulfillable fantasy of the perpetuation of perfection and of ultimately acquiring the oedipal parent of the opposite sex. From the point of view of male-female differentiation by the end of adolescence, such a freedom from the oedipal parents also means freedom from oedipal guilt and hatred and the ability to possess a functioning penis or vagina without feeling it as deficient or abnormal.

In the first part of adolescence, the fear of oedipal aggression and the continued fear of the parents' envy result in a cautious acquisition psychically of one's own sexually mature genitals. During this period there is still a defensive need to give this up and temporarily to become passive again in relation to the oedipal parent of the same sex. This temporary passivity or submission contains the young adolescent's anxiety and fear of retaliation from the oedipal parent of the opposite sex, while simultaneously expressing his wish to remain cared for and loved in a nonincestuous—that is, nonconflictual—way. Normally, the oedipal identification with the parent of the same sex enables the adolescent to overcome this regressive pull.

Only in the latter part of adolescence is the body image sufficiently stable and integrated for the adolescent to be able to give up the defensive use of passive submission to the oedipal parents as a source of gratification. This then enables the adolescent unconsciously to be free to replace this earlier relationship by actively seeking an object relationship with a person of the opposite sex.

In seeking such a relationship, the adolescent is unconsciously confronted with the need to integrate the presence of the genitals of the opposite sex. Normal development proceeds when a mental representation of the genitals of the opposite sex has been indestructibly internalized, a representation which contains simultaneously the basis for the potential of narcissistic union and libidinal gratification. It is only then that an object relationship with a person of the opposite sex can replace the autoerotic activity that, until then, was used for "trial action." Such a development then allows for identification with the person of the opposite sex, one which is then the basis for object love (Abraham 1924).

Such a normal outcome is expressed by the adolescent's freedom to seek and find peers of the same and opposite sexes, where developmentally those of the same sex act as objects for identification and those of the opposite sex act as objects of the sexual wishes. But now, this process represents the ability, once more, to experience the anxiety of the separateness of one's own body, while also being able to maintain the fantasy of reunion through intercourse (Deutsch 1932; Ferenczi 1913). By the end of adolescence, this normal process results in the ultimate differentiation of oneself as male or female.

This outcome is, however, not available to the adolescent who has experienced a developmental breakdown. In development that is unable to proceed to a heterosexual object relationship, but remains homosexual, perverse, or autoerotic, the integration of the mental representation of the genitals of the opposite sex continues to be defended against and experienced as a source of anxiety. In such instances, puberty is experienced instead as a demand to give up past perfections, a demand to acquire genital characteristics that would destroy the relationships to the oedipal objects, or, in the more severe cases, a feeling that puberty is the final confrontation with the fact that the body is different from what the adolescent hoped it would be. This would then represent for the adolescent the confirmation of the mother's hatred of the child.

The meaning of the breakdown or psychopathology now present in the adolescent patient's life is contained in certain fantasies that are an integral part of his daily life and activities. In the previous chapter, we referred to the patient's central masturbation fantasy, which contains the various regressive satisfactions and the main sexual identifications. We have in mind the existence of a hierarchy of fantasies, with the implication that there is one core fantasy that has meaning and power beyond other fantasies and that is ultimately woven into the pathology.[2] This fantasy has the characteristic of being directly linked to the oedipus complex in that its form and content are fixed with the oedipal resolution. But only in adolescence is it finally integrated into the *sexual* body image, also carrying with it the direction of the person's sexual relationships and gratifications. Such clinical evidence has led us to the assumption that the image of one's own body, which has been organized by the end of the phallic-oedipal period, determines the form of oedipal resolution and remains central to a person's later sexual life and psychopathology.

2. For a fuller discussion, see chapter 1.

What is subsumed under this assumption is the following: During the phallic-oedipal period—that is, between the ages of three and five—the child becomes more fully aware of the differences between phallic and castrated, and this precursor of later male-female differentiation ushers in the need to deal with his or her incestuous wishes. When Freud referred to the superego as the heir to the oedipus complex (1924), we believe he meant something well beyond the idea of an agency in the mind being set up that takes over the parental strictures and ideals and makes them part of the child's own internal world. By "resolution" he meant the unconscious compromise that satisfies a number of masters—id, external reality, and the awareness of one's own helplessness in the face of the oedipal father or mother. Resolution means, therefore, the internal reality that one's own body is now separate from the bodies of the parents but is still helpless to fulfill the sexual role in reality. The superego may safeguard the child's ego, but resolution of the oedipus complex means that there is a unification and an integration of the prephallic and phallic body representations. We now begin to see developmentally the outcome of infantile sexuality, which takes into account the cathexis of the body, the relation to the mother, and the preoedipal—that is, nonincestuous—gratifications from this relationship to the mother and to one's own body (Loewald 1979).

But "oedipal resolution" also implies the ultimate narcissistic cathexis of the sexual body image, which means that the preoedipal relationships and internalizations are now emotionally experienced as love or hatred for one's own phallic or castrated body. In other words, the earlier feelings of love and hatred from the parents become part of the love or the hatred by the child of his own body, now experienced as phallic or as castrated. For the first time in the person's life, he experiences his own body as the source or reservoir of his love or hatred, containing those objects who love or hate, protect or threaten. In adolescence, this is seen in the severe disorders in self-hatred, in the need to destroy the sexual body, in the efforts to change the body or the image of the body after puberty, or in the feeling that the persecutors are ultimately housed in one's own body.

When introducing the assumption about the body image and its relation to the oedipal resolution, we referred to the central masturbation fantasy. Although this fantasy exists in preoedipal life as well, or so it seems, it is only during the phallic-oedipal period that an incestuous, as distinct from a sexual, meaning is added. But only after puberty, however, we see the addition in some patients of the feeling of being compelled to behave in specific ways, with the unconscious awareness that they are no longer in control of the fantasy and its related activities. In other words, the defense against the oedipal wish becomes precarious, and a break with external reality as well as a distortion of the image of their own sexual body may be the only means left for them to contain their incestuous wish.

The compelling quality that is added to this fantasy after puberty in some people could be explained as representing the failure to accommodate the change from the earlier phallic or castrated image of the body to that of male or female, masculine or feminine. In other words, the phallus or the vagina is normally experienced as an active or potentially active organ only after puberty. With the arrival of puberty, the person experiences the need to integrate the functioning penis or the functioning vagina as part of the representation of the body. And with the presence of the functioning penis or vagina, the earlier means of dealing with one's incestuous wishes and fears creates a demand on the ego which has never before been experienced. The earlier fantasies of incest and parricide can become a reality now, and so can oedipal revenge (Loewald 1979).

DEVELOPMENTAL BREAKDOWN AND THE OEDIPUS COMPLEX

Freud's insight that every human being, at a certain developmental period, fantasied the destruction or removal of one parent so that the child could acquire the sole sexual love of the remaining parent led him to insights about the meaning of conflict and defense and to an understanding of the later male-female differentiation. He could now explain incest and parricide not as passing fantasies that were the misfortune of a few but as processes to which he gave a central place in human life, especially in understanding the range of pathologies we meet in our clinical work.

Freud went well beyond this oft-repeated description of the child's wishes and intentions. He wanted to convey by this concept a process of development, starting with the infant's relationship to and identification with his mother, whereby the infant begins to see his own body as an object from which he can obtain gratification and through which the initial skeleton of ego functions begin to develop, including ultimately the development and formation of the superego. He maintained that the oedipus complex as a developmental landmark could be conceptualized as taking place only at the time of the phallic phase; in other words, for him it was a concept that had meaning only if one took for granted a fundamental unity or interdependence between the biology and the psychology of the individual (1924). The oedipus complex had to be tied to a period of libidinal and ego development when sufficient differentiation had taken place between the child's own body and the object with which the child identified, when the child's relationship to his own body carried with it an image of the body in the child's mind, and when sexual longing was accompanied unconsciously by emotions that made this wish and this urgency into a state of jealousy, hatred, and love, together with a simultaneous feeling that the parent who was hated would retaliate by withdrawing love and also by physically attacking and damaging the child—the classical situation of the child's castration anxiety.

An important aspect of the theory about the oedipus complex is that it is the culmination of a long process whose primary result, in developmental terms, is that the ego now must act as an organizing and unifying agent of all of one's past, while at the same time adding a new agency of the mind that would contain the parents of the past and the real and fanta-

sied approvals and criticisms and threats of the past, but on a
level of functioning beyond the original crude wishes and fears
associated with the period before the oedipus complex. With
the resolution of the oedipus complex, infantile sexuality
would begin to be left behind—that is, the child was now becoming an organized and, at times, a very troubled being. Om-
nipotence would now be dented by a new sense of reality, including a new sense of internal reality.

When Freud put forward the concept of the oedipus complex, he was well aware of the significance of preoedipal life, as
is shown by his writings on infantile masturbation (1905), his
theory of narcissism (1914), the idea of forepleasure as compared with that of endpleasure, the theme of finding an object
after puberty and his statement that it is in fact a refinding of
an object, and his innumerable references to the central significance of the infant's and child's relationship to the mother, to
the breast, and to the connection between this and the child's
earliest efforts to establish the differences between internal and
external reality (1923). His dialogues which have been reported
with Breuer, Jung, Abraham, Ferenczi, and Jones elaborate
this (see Jones 1954, 1955, 1957). But Freud did not know
what we know now about the preoedipal period. The significance of the contributions about preoedipal life (Jacobson
1964; Kernberg 1979; Klein 1945, 1958; Mahler, Pine, and
Bergman 1975; Segal 1964, 1977; Winnicott 1953, 1958) is that
they enlarge our knowledge about the precursors of normal
and pathological development and give us possible insights into
the critical developmental differences that contribute to an outcome in the adult of neurosis or psychosis, perversion, or the
borderline and narcissistic pathologies.

But these pathologies of the adult become fixed only after
the sexual body image has been unified—that is, only during
adolescence when the original oedipal body image of "phallic"
or "castrated" becomes a sexual body image of "male" or "female." In this sense, Freud's view of adolescence as a recapitu-
lation of the person's earlier life, now experienced within the
context of a physically mature body, takes on a special significance for understanding developmental breakdown. Although

we do not, at this point, have sufficient clinical evidence, it seems likely that the developmental breakdown at puberty as expressed in the reaction to being sexually male or female is the counterpart of the original reaction to one's body as being either phallic or castrated.

CLINICAL MATERIAL: Jane

The clinical material illustrates the connection between the psychopathology observed during an analysis of an adolescent and the assumptions about acute developmental breakdown and male-female differentiation. This material shows the link between the patient's present pathology and the factors that seem to have been important in the organization of the image of her body by the end of the phallic-oedipal period and ultimately in determining her oedipal resolution.

Jane was in analysis from the age of seventeen to twenty-four, having come for treatment after a sudden serious episode at school where she started yelling and attacked other students.[3] Although this might have been considered to be the first sign of an acute developmental breakdown, it became obvious during her treatment that the breakdown had really taken place quietly at about the time of puberty, when she began to feel compelled to have intercourse and became convinced that somebody would one day kill her—a belief that was a persistent issue in the transference—that is, of feeling that the analyst did not care for her and really wanted her to die.

Her oedipal relationships seem to have been characterized by an underlying feeling of revenge—her revenge on her younger sister and on her mother, or her mother's revenge on her for being her father's favorite and for being able to get him to do whatever she wished. In latency and for a short time in adolescence, this fantasied seduction of her father was lived out, and perhaps contributed to by the father. Jane spent time with him in bed, for example, cuddling him and believing that she was able to get him to have an erection. Jane believed that

3. A more detailed description of Jane's analysis is contained in chapter 9.

her mother's talk of suicide and depression were due to Jane's ability to destroy her mother's relationship with her father.

But this not uncommon fantasy of the oedipal girl had another component which seems to have been important in the psychopathology that was observed late in her adolescence and early in her adulthood and enacted in a suicide attempt soon after her analysis began. For as long as she could recall, Jane felt that she had something inside her that could kill people or could turn on herself and kill her. In adolescence, this became manifest in her belief that her vagina was filled with pus or poison. In intercourse, Jane believed that, while the man thought that she was giving him pleasure, she was able to destroy his penis by the poison in her vagina.

But this also had another, more important meaning for her later life. Jane secretly believed that she and her mother together could effectively destroy anybody, and by "destroy" she meant kill. Her identification with and hatred of her mother were disguised by her unremitting feeling that she, Jane, must either die or be killed, a feeling that was partially lived out in her hitchhiking experiences in adolescence, during which she came near to being raped or even murdered.

But it was her central masturbation fantasy that gave the most reliable clues to some of her psychopathology and to her breakdown in adolescence—a fantasy that took the analyst a long time to put together from a range of activities, from dreams, and from the transference. "There is a little man inside her who forces her to masturbate, after which she has the shameful fantasy of being caught by a man who gets her to massage his body and suck his penis. She then curls up so that her mouth and her vagina are touching."

For as long as she could remember, Jane believed that she was never quite right as a female. This doubt contained her fear of and wish for lesbian relationships, but more important was her feeling that the hatred she felt for her mother could never permit her to do anything other than destroy the man's penis. The "little man" in her fantasy represented her father, but also the "little man" was her personification of her own disowned aggression, expressed by her belief of pus or poison in her vagina.

Of the greatest importance to 'an understanding of her pathology was the fact that it was her vagina, rather than any other part of her body, that she felt contained all her destructiveness and hatred. The preoedipal relationship to the mother and the identification with the mother were portrayed by the idea of the mouth and the vagina touching—that is, of the mouth poisoning the vagina and vice versa and also in the fantasy of the man getting her to suck his penis. At the appropriate times in the analysis and in the transference, this could be understood in terms of the patient's relationship to her own fantasied penis or to the fantasy of her mother's breast as poisonous and destructive and of the mother as the one responsible for giving Jane this poison. The importance for this patient's development and for *her relationship to herself as a woman*, as seen in adolescence and in young adulthood, is that her oedipal relationships (and ultimately her oedipal resolution) were dependent on her symbolic use of her vagina as the reservoir of all her hatred.

The analyst assumed that this was the reason her psychopathology, as expressed by her acute breakdown in adolescence and then by her suicide attempt, manifested itself in the way it did. From puberty, Jane seemed to believe unconsciously that she could destroy whomever she chose and that her vagina was the tormentor of others as well as of herself. Her guilt about what she was able to do, together with her hatred of that part of her body that made her female, led her to try to kill herself. When these factors were concentrated within the transference, it became possible for Jane to see how compelled she was to destroy that part of her own body that contained her incestuous wish or, perhaps more correctly, would enable her to carry out that wish.

If this case had been understood mainly in preoedipal terms, treatment would have avoided the working through of the oedipal fantasy of destruction by the use of the vagina and would have encouraged Jane to encapsulate her sexual disorder by keeping her feelings about her vagina split off from consciousness. It might have resulted in some insight as to her motivation and put her in touch with a part of her past, but there would have been little change in her relationships to men or to herself as a woman. The pathology would likely have found other ways of expression, but her vagina would have remained poisonous and destructive, and her image of herself as a poisonous female would have persisted.

3
The Body Image and Masturbation

In our assessment and treatment of seriously disturbed adolescents, we became aware that the study of masturbation and change in body image holds important clues to the meaning of sudden and severe disruptions in development at puberty. Such disruptions, which we have referred to as developmental breakdown, mean an interference in the integration of the sexual body image during adolescence and the likely move to established psychopathology by the end of adolescence. We felt that such a study might also yield insight into some of the critical differences between those adolescents whose development proceeds normally and those whose development does not.

Many writers, beginning with Freud (1923), have described the critical place of the relationship to one's own body in the development of the mental apparatus. They have also stressed the close link between the body image and the development of ego functions, in particular, perception and reality testing— two functions that are commonly impaired in adolescents who have experienced a developmental breakdown (Bak 1939; Blos 1967; Federn 1952; Freud 1923; Greenacre 1953; Hoffer 1950; Jacobson 1964; Mahler 1963; Peto 1959; Schilder 1935; Winnicott 1953).

The role of masturbation in development and in psychopathology has been investigated in a limited way with the main emphasis on the nature of the conflict around masturbation and on the place of fantasy (Deutsch 1968; Eissler 1958; Francis 1968; A. Freud 1949; Freud 1905; Jacobson 1964; Lampl-de Groot 1950). In a 1920 footnote to his "Three Essays"

(1905) Freud noted what we have observed among adolescents —a relevant observation that adds a dimension to the idea that adolescence recapitulates the past in a prescribed way. He said, "The most general and most important factor concerned must no doubt be that masturbation represents the executive agency of the whole of infantile sexuality and is, therefore, able to take over the sense of guilt attaching to it" (p. 189).

In this chapter, we concentrate on the role that masturbation and masturbation fantasies play in enabling the adolescent to establish the primacy of genitality and on the internal factors that determine whether or not the adolescent will succeed in changing the image of his body to include his physically mature genitals as functioning organs. We have often been faced with the need to decide whether the behavior or fantasies adolescents reported were part of normal adolescence or contained the core of their pathology. Some adolescent patients reported masturbation fantasies that sounded regressive in nature but did not seem to interfere seriously with their social and sexual adaptation. Others presented a much more organized picture but nevertheless felt that they had reached a deadlock in their development. They experienced their masturbation or masturbation fantasies as repeated proof that something was seriously wrong with them (and their assessments were often correct).

Such differences in the extent and quality of anxiety experienced by adolescents over masturbation and masturbation fantasies made us think that we might be observing the pathological side of something that in normal adolescence serves the important function of helping the ego reorganize itself around the supremacy of genitality. In the adolescents described in this chapter, the deadlock they felt they had reached represented their awareness that they were unable to use masturbation or masturbation fantasies as something equivalent to "trial action." Not only was genitality dangerous to them but the prephallic fantasies (even though these were ego-alien) offered such satisfaction that they severely hindered development. The very nature of these regressive fantasies prevented their use as "trial action" for adult sexual behavior.

MASTURBATION AS "TRIAL ACTION"

Masturbation and masturbation fantasies during adolescence normally act as an autoerotic activity, which helps to integrate regressive fantasies as part of the effort to achieve genital dominance. The adolescent's oedipal fantasies can be allowed into consciousness, but in a disguised form, and are then normally re-repressed. Some adolescents cannot use masturbation and the accompanying fantasies in this way but instead experience masturbation or the fantasies as a loss of body control or as passive submission to a force within themselves over which they feel powerless. Masturbation in adolescence not only serves the function of an action that is experienced within the safety of one's own thoughts, it is also a way of testing which sexual thoughts, feelings, or gratifications are acceptable to the superego and which are unacceptable and therefore must not be allowed to become part of the person's image of himself or herself as a sexually mature male or female. The problem for the adolescent is not simply which parts of the fantasy or which regressive wishes in general are acceptable and which have to be rejected; rather, for the first time in his life, the adolescent is faced with the adequacy or inadequacy of the defensive organization to help him deal with these problems. He may now feel that he has little ability to defend against certain regressive pulls which, if gratified, would not be acceptable to him and for which he may be severely punished by the superego. In some adolescents, temporary regression produces acute anxiety because they fear they may not be able to reestablish their previous level of functioning. Temporary regression means, for some adolescents, allowing into consciousness those fantasies and accompanying wishes that represent abnormality but that, at the same time, they may want to gratify.

OWNERSHIP OF THE BODY

In each of the adolescents described in this chapter certain pre-oedipal experiences had disturbed the oedipal solution in such a way that genitality would inevitably be disrupted. This distortion was, in adolescence, then fought out within themselves around the question of "ownership of the body." One important factor seems to be whether the adolescent can emotionally experience his mature body as belonging to himself or reacts as if his body still belonged to his mother, who first cared for it. These adolescents felt that in masturbation and accompanying fantasies they were reliving a real experience, which included the satisfaction of regressive wishes. They were unable to break with this pattern and felt they had no control over their bodies, which they regarded as their enemies or as something quite separate from the rest of themselves. In their need to create the feeling that their bodies were either nonexistent or free of danger, they resorted to various means—suicide attempts, drug taking, compulsive eating. They experienced masturbation (which Freud called the "primary addiction" [1897, 272]) or masturbation fantasies as equivalent to a failure in repression or as the vehicle for the satisfaction of something perverse and shameful. Not one of them was able to use masturbation and the fantasies constructively to further development to adulthood, as in establishing heterosexual object relationships or the primacy of the genitals.

CLINICAL MATERIAL

The first obvious and undeniable sign that something is seriously wrong frequently occurs soon after puberty. When we then look at the adolescent's history more closely, we generally detect signs of earlier pathology. A colleague has observed that a number of adolescents admitted to the acute ward of a mental hospital "broke down" following their first emission or soon after the beginning of menstruation. When these patients were asked about their immediate fear or panic, they explained it on the basis of their "confusion," or they said that certain feelings drove them mad. Sometimes, more specifically, they said that they either wished for intercourse with the parent of the opposite sex or became terrified by the thought that they would kill one of their parents.

This observation is an extreme version of what occurs in the minds of many normal adolescents. In adolescents who show signs of severe disorder, we can observe the failure in the defense organization that normally keeps the oedipal and preoedipal fantasies or wishes under repression—a failure that leads to the adolescent's ego suddenly being overwhelmed. We can explain some of these manifestations as the ego's inability to deal with the quantitative and qualitative changes in the instinctual demands taking place at puberty; as a result what is normally an unconscious fantasy may now become either a conscious thought or, worse, an action. If the break is not totally psychotic, the adolescent will become terrified, and his behavior will portray a combination of confusion and fear.

We have begun with a rather extreme example of a breakdown because of its relevance to understanding the change in the relationship to the physical body and to the image of the body that must take place following the onset of puberty. We believe that in such cases several factors are at work—dissociation from one's physically mature body; sudden collapse of the oedipal identifications; failure of the defenses against the oedipal aggression and the accompanying fantasies of destruction, incest, and hatred of one's own body. The guilt inherent in this process may help explain the suicides and attempted suicides of some adolescents, which we believe are aggressive attacks on the internalized parent and at the same time are attacks on the person's own body, at that moment experienced as separate from the rest of oneself and as not belonging to oneself. For some adolescents, dying means killing the body but not necessarily the mind.

In the following histories of two adolescent patients (Alan and Susan) who made suicide attempts, a central feature is the extent to which they dissociated their minds from their bodies and the sensations arising in their bodies. Both felt that they must not have feelings, and both viewed the internalized mother as the person responsible for the control of their feelings. Both felt that their mothers were giving them permission to experience feelings; but they also felt that their mothers could withdraw this permission at any time, and then the sexually mature body and its sensations had to be disowned. Although these feelings represented an early disruption of the relationship between mother and child, it signified also the present unconscious wish of the adolescent to disown the sexual body, expressed now by the projection of the hatred of the sexual body on to the mother. This hatred of the mother was more available to consciousness than was the underlying wish to submit passively and to remain nonsexual.

One of the patients, Susan, used to talk of her body as that "filthy, ugly, horrible mass which is attached to me." In early adolescence, following the onset of menstruation and the growth of large breasts (the size of her breasts was very important to her—no matter what she did or how she dressed she could not hide them), she had her first breakdown in the form of lying in bed for three months. At that time her body was "tired," but she felt that masturbation had confirmed that she was horrible. While she was in bed her mother took over the care of her body—something Susan encouraged and wanted to perpetuate. In her recollection one of the "lovely things" about staying in bed was that she could just lie there and think—she did not feel anything, her body was being looked after by her mother. Later in adolescence she formed a lesbian relationship, which was satisfactory as long as she could feel that this relationship was a "meeting of two minds" while her body was "available" to the other girl. She could never accept the fact that the guilt she felt had anything to do with her recent behavior. She had to continue to keep the body and its sensations separate from her mind.

When these patients described their masturbatory activities after puberty, it became clear that masturbation represented a perpetual demand by the body to feel something that they had attempted to deny. In their experience, the fantasies which accompanied masturbation confirmed their worthlessness or abnormality, and the pleasure or satisfaction they derived from masturbation was wrong and should be eliminated or destroyed in some way. While they seemed to be aware of an ongoing internal battle, they could not alter their attitudes to their bodies or to the sensations coming from their bodies. Masturbation and the accompanying fantasies were never experienced as trial actions—instead the masturbation carried into consciousness the distorted oedipal fantasies, which encouraged further regression. For this reason, their masturbation and the fantasies had to be experienced as ego-alien.

The material of the adolescents who tried to reject their bodies or the body sensations contained a repetitive theme: masturbation, or even a pleasurable feeling in their genitals, either was a confrontation with their abnormality or represented their being forced by some unknown or uncontrollable power to give up an earlier state of equilibrium. It was as if puberty had suddenly changed the body into an enemy. Yet, in every instance in which the period before adolescence was worshipped or longed for, it turned out that the patient's suffering during latency had been severe. The difference in the experience of childhood and adolescence was that in childhood the patient was able to find some means of avoiding the stress, whereas in adolescence the reality of having a physically mature body forced him to fight his body and bodily feelings.

In each of the following cases, the masturbatory activities and accompanying fantasies disclosed that these adolescents had reached an intrapsychic deadlock. Their need to keep their body sensations separate from their image of themselves as sexually mature was proof that the integration of the physically mature genitals as part of the postpubertal body image was severely handicapped.

Alan

Alan was referred for treatment at the age of eighteen following a suicide attempt. He had an outstanding academic record. Six months prior to referral, a friend had invited him to a party. The prospect of meeting girls socially made Alan anxious, but he nevertheless accepted the invitation. At the party he could not allow himself to dance with a girl who he thought was attractive. When he got home, he was miserable and angry. He felt there must be things in life other than girls, parties, or sex. When he awoke the next morning, he decided to kill himself, without thinking too much about it. He swallowed a poisonous substance that he had kept hidden for months, "just in case I needed it."

A central theme in his treatment was the question of whether it is right to do something actively to bring about an emission. When he had a nocturnal emission, he felt that it had nothing to do with him; whereas to masturbate would mean that he had decided to ejaculate. Throughout latency and early adolescence he refused to recognize that his body had any needs at all—it was as if eating, sleeping, and defecating were habits or reflex actions. When he had his first nocturnal emission, he was furious with his body for tricking him into producing semen. In early adolescence he tried to masturbate but did not feel anything in his penis. Although this worried him, it also relieved him because it proved that "the body is the body, and it's got nothing to do with me."

Alan was the only child of unhappy parents. He remembered his father as a withdrawn, depressed, and ignorant man. According to Alan, he and his father had almost nothing to do with each other. This was similar to his mother's attitude toward his father. The parents had had separate bedrooms for as long as Alan could remember. Alan and his mother spent all their time together, while the father lived what seemed to be a totally separate existence.

Among the many intimacies and bodily routines between Alan and his mother in childhood, one seemed to be especially significant: the mother had regularly wiped Alan's anus after defecation. He insisted that she do this until there was no sign of feces on the paper. But suddenly, around the age of seven or eight, he refused to let anybody else perform this task and undertook it himself, sometimes spending ten minutes wiping himself and using as much as half a roll of paper. Various recollections of his latency indicate that this was the central theme of his primal-scene fantasy—that is, one partner does something to the other partner via the anus. This fantasy also contained his fear of and wish for anal penetration. There was great confusion in his mind about the proper roles of the male and the female, with a belief that it might be the woman (with the phallus) who penetrates the man.

This fantasy also contained his hatred and fear of the mother. At this point in his adolescence, he felt tied to her, even though he sometimes imagined that if he let himself go he could kill her.

The suicide attempt, then, can be understood in this context. He remembered that after he came home from the party, he had wondered what it might be like to have intercourse with one of the girls he had met. He was convinced that he would never succeed. He was frightened that he would completely lose control—as if it might turn out to be catastrophic for him. He thought he would have to do something drastic to succeed, and suicide seemed to him to be the answer. In treatment the analyst established that the suicide would simultaneously have enabled Alan to destroy and rid himself of the hated internalized mother and would have done away with his weak and ineffectual body. But he never thought it would mean *his* death—it meant only the death of his body. Prior to his suicide attempt Alan had occasionally speculated about whether something could be done about his body, and he had had the fantasy that if he killed his body he might become alive again with a new and properly functioning body.

Susan

Susan came to analysis after suffering a breakdown at the university. The tutors had been worried that she might kill herself, so she was admitted to a hospital. Susan sought treatment soon after she graduated with distinction. She was twenty-one when treatment began. After fifteen months she discontinued her treatment.

Throughout her life, Susan had been considered brilliant, and her mother had always insisted that Susan's mind be developed. To Susan, her mind made her much better than her younger brother. Yet, while she saw no advantage in being a man, to be a female was abhorrent and made her feel worthless. In early adolescence, she masturbated a great deal with the fantasy that either a man or another woman was making love to her through some kind of anal penetration. During masturbation she would feel wild, crazy, and wonderful—all at the same time. At times she masturbated anally or crouched down as if she were defecating. She would always feel terrible afterward and often hoped she would die.

As mentioned earlier, she went to bed for three months in early adolescence, during which time her mother took care of her. In a lesbian relationship she established when she was seventeen, she and the other girl would hold or kiss or masturbate each other. At that time Susan believed it might be possible to live happily with this girl. When this girl started a relationship with a boy, Susan was distressed to the point of considering suicide.

As a child, and even during her adolescence, Susan was convinced that her body was not quite complete. In adolescence, she could not allow boys to come close to her. She could not bear the reality of having a vagina—this would be equivalent to giving up hope that she could in some way alter her body. She was convinced that her mother had done something to her body and that if she renounced sexual feelings she might be allowed to have a complete body. Sexual feelings were a "demand and a curse on me," because they jeopardized the defense against the hatred of the mother for giving her such a useless and incomplete body.

According to Susan her mother thought of her as being much better than her brother—she had an outstanding mind, she could create with her mind, she did not have to be like other children. She was something "special," which for Susan meant that she must not be preoccupied by sexual thoughts or wishes. During her adolescence, the body-mind split was strengthened by the need to keep her perverse masturbation fantasies separate from her mind—as if she were not responsible for these fantasies, even though the guilt she experienced was enormous. At the same time, this body-mind split helped temporarily in her defense against the extreme aggression directed at the mother. But this precarious balance was upset when she reached puberty and, for the first time, her perverse masturbation fantasies became conscious. Masturbation then confirmed that her body was dirty and worthless, while gratifying in fantasy her perverse wishes. Moreover, it was equivalent to a failure in her efforts to keep repressed the wish to destroy her body, which also meant the destruction of the mother.

Something went seriously wrong in the adolescent development of these patients. Each of them, no matter what he or she did, felt "stuck." Each described his or her entire adolescence as very painful. In both cases, puberty seemed to set in motion a constant battle with something inside themselves over which they felt they had no control. These adolescents experienced their masturbation either as a confirmation of their abnormality or as a threat to their whole ego functioning, especially to their defensive organization.

Two recurrent themes were especially clear in the masturbation fantasies. First, they hated their bodies for forcing this activity on them; and second, they felt helpless in the face of the abnormal fantasies, which inevitably would bring about a feeling of worthlessness and guilt. Hatred of the body was for them equivalent to hatred of the internalized parent.

Although the fantasies and attitudes of these adolescents to their bodies could be viewed simply as representing defensive efforts against the positive oedipal wishes, something else occurred that produced this deadlock and strengthened the need to disown their bodies and body sensations: The onset of puberty apparently endangered the earlier defense against the aggression directed at the mother. When this aggression was reactivated in adolescence, it was experienced as something that could at any time take over and be put into action. Masturbation and the accompanying fantasies were further threats to these adolescents because the ensuing regression acted as a constant confirmation of their hatred and their abnormality. The mother, who originally was the stimulator and protector of the child's body, was now regarded as the persecutor (A. Freud 1965; Hoffer 1950; Winnicott 1953). Susan believed that her mother would "die of shame" if she knew what her "special child" was doing or thinking. Alan was convinced that his mother was watching him when he had a nocturnal emission and that he could never get away from her no matter how horrible he was to her.

Adolescents whose development has proceeded along more normal lines usually manage to keep their preoedipal, regressed fantasies under repression and, during masturbation, allow into consciousness only the more acceptable heterosexual fantasies that usually involve an appropriate love object. In treatment, it is often possible to undo some of the repression and to locate the regressed or perverse fantasies that may be present. But the mere existence of these fantasies is not a sign of abnormality. While such fantasies may act as a threat, they are normally well defended against and remain unconscious. But the adolescents we have described reacted differently to their masturbation and the accompanying fantasies. The regressed fantasies were felt to be perverse and intruded into consciousness. When these were experienced in relation to a physically mature body, the fantasy was nearly equivalent to an action. The fantasy felt real and dangerous.

This formulation—that the onset of puberty endangers the earlier defense against the aggression directed at the mother—seems to apply to both male and female adolescents. However, the meaning of the preoedipal and oedipal aggression directed at the mother is not the same for the male and the female child, with the implication that the resulting pathology will be different for the male and the female adolescent. The content of the masturbation fantasies enables us to reconstruct the child's conception of the primal scene and to determine which parent he or she is identified with.

In the case of Alan, his sense of helplessness in the face of his sexual sensations and the feeling of being completely overpowered following ejaculation served the function of denying his extreme castration anxiety by enabling him to feel identified with his mother. He lived out the fantasy of being like the mother with the phallus, a fantasy which also contained the notion that the mother's possession of a phallus made her more acceptable to the father. On a preoedipal level, there was the wish to be cared for, and this perpetuated the relationship to the mother. But in order to understand his pathology in adolescence, it is necessary to view the conflict mainly in oedipal terms—that is, his masturbation and the fantasy contain the identification with his mother who, he believed, had a phallus. The maintenance of this fantasy in adolescence allowed him to feel that his body was more like the mother's than the father's. Greenacre's formulations about the development of the body image (1953, 1958, 1960), especially the faulty development in fetishism, are relevant in this context.

Susan, however, regarded her mother as the castrator as well as the protector. The beginning of menstruation confirmed that her body was no good, and sexual feelings in adolescence simply reminded her of how horrible her body was. At the same time, she felt that her mother knew everything about her, as if her mother was with her all the time. To touch her genitals meant that she had to recognize that her mother had given her a body that was useless and abnormal. The onset of menstruation destroyed the identification with the mother with the phallus because it suddenly forced Susan to give up her belief that her body would change. Masturbation represented an additional danger because it confirmed the fact of her damaged body and thereby aroused the aggression against the mother. It is precisely this aggression that in turn tied Susan so completely to her mother.

4
The Female Adolescent, the Relationship to the Body, and Masturbation

In the previous chapter, we discussed the contribution of masturbation to the integration of the sexual body image in adolescence. But, as is generally the case in a discussion of masturbation, the concentration has been on its role in the development of the male. However, during the treatment of female adolescents it became clear that masturbation evoked a conflict different from the one usually experienced by male adolescents and that after puberty masturbation had a different significance in the development of the relationship to the body for the female adolescent than for the male.

We have described masturbation as having an essential and positive function in the move toward normal adulthood for the adolescent boy, but it does not seem to have the same role in the adolescent girl's sexual development. This would imply that there may be important differences in the development of the male adolescent's and the female adolescent's relationship to the sexually mature body—differences that have implications in defining normal and pathological development. Freud attributed the relative absence of masturbation in the little girl to her experiencing disappointment in her lack of a penis when she begins to compare her genitals with those of the boy—an explanation still controversial among analysts.

Before discussing an alternative explanation for the relative absence of masturbation in girls who are nevertheless developing normally, we would ask the question differently. Is it normal for the girl to give up masturbation during the oedipal or

latency periods or during adolescence, or, as some writers seem
to imply, is its lack in an adolescent girl or a woman indicative
of earlier repression—one that analysis should succeed in lift-
ing? Clinical discussions often report that a female patient had
"become able" to masturbate. Rarely has it been questioned
whether this is a sign of a normal, progressive move and, if not,
what the meaning of it might be.

THE FIRST PHASE OF MASTURBATION

In "Three Essays" (1905) Freud was not specific in dating the
first phase of masturbation, but he described the second phase
of masturbation as being oedipal. From this we conclude that
the first phase refers to the preoedipal period. The first phase
of masturbation thus encompasses the period during which the
relationship to one's own body is formed, and this is originally
expressed and later symbolically experienced in the relationship of the hand to the body. The symbolic meaning of the
hand takes on a conflictual significance for the adolescent girl,
and this is the conflict we see as responsible for the girl's inability to use masturbation developmentally in the same way as the
adolescent boy does.

   Lindner's (1879) observation that the infant's thumb-sucking
has an erotic component provided Freud with the basis for the-
oretical formulations concerning the developmental significance of masturbation in the total spectrum of sexual activity,
thus enabling Freud to extend the concept of sexuality beyond
that of genital sexuality. He showed that the erotic satisfaction
the infant experiences in thumb-sucking (1905, 179) implies
the existence of an oral sexual drive with the breast as its object
and that the mother (in her function of caring for the infant's
body) acts as both seducer and frustrator of the child's other
libidinally determined wishes (such as being held, kept warm,
and fondled). The breast is first experienced as a frustrating
object through the experience of its absence. The infant is able
to negate this aspect of the breast by finding that a part of its

own body can be used to create the fantasy of the absent object and, in this way, to undo the frustrating experience.[1]

Here we place the emphasis on the infant's experience of its own body as having the capacity for gratification. The activity of the thumb in relation to the infant's mouth repeats and becomes identified with the mother's active satisfying relationship to the infant. Subsequently, the activity of the whole hand in relation to the child's body is a repetition of the experience of the activity of the mother's hand in relation to the child (Kris 1951). All masturbatory activity contains the duality of both an active and a passive experience. During this first phase of masturbation, while the infant is progressively feeling its body as separate from the mother's, the activity of the thumb in relation to the mouth and later of the hand in relation to the body and genitals provides the basis for the child's progressive separation of its own body image from that of the mother's and for the beginning relationship to its own body via the mother's activity in relation to the child's body. This identification enables the child to undo the experience of separation by feeling more in control of the satisfaction of preoedipal wishes through the use of its own body. But the unconscious identification of her own hand with that of the mother's subsequently becomes a source of conflict for the little girl, when the hand is used during masturbation.

By limiting our observations to female masturbation, we can focus on an important difference among female children, adolescent girls, and adult women. We know from clinical observation that only some girls and women masturbate; the difference between those who do and those who do not can now be defined more specifically as being between those who use their hands to touch their genitals and those who do not. Writers who use clinical material to show that female children use other means for obtaining sexual excitement (such as thigh pressure or fecal retention) and conclude that there is no basic differ-

1. The significance of the simultaneous nature of the infant's experience of two separate parts of its own body—the hand and mouth—for the formation of a separate body image has been discussed by Hoffer (1949).

ence between females and males in the developmental significance of masturbation, do not sufficiently consider the meaning to the child of the different means used by them to masturbate (see Sherfey 1966). We see some women's avoidance of the use of the hand for masturbation as characterizing the difference between male and female. There are boys who avoid using their hands to touch the penis for masturbatory purposes; however, for boys, as different from girls, this avoidance is always a sign of disturbance in development.

In his paper on "Female Sexuality" (1931) Freud points out that the girl's relinquishing of masturbation—which he saw as occurring at the end of her long period of attachment to her mother—could not be viewed simply as a result of prohibitions coming from the external world. Prohibitions, he pointed out, can just as easily lead to a defiant need to cling to an activity. Freud's explanation was that the relinquishment must therefore be internally determined—that is, by the child's experience of disappointment with her own body. Irrespective of the unconscious content of that disappointment, this observation has been confirmed by analysts in clinical work with children and adults. But why this disappointment is expressed by avoidance of touching the genitals seems less clear.

Many analysts (Horney 1933; Jones 1927; Klein 1928) find unconvincing the explanation that the satisfaction the girl obtains is no longer sufficient because of the fantasy of what could be experienced if she had a penis. It can be understood instead as the girl's giving up of an active relationship to her own body when she is forced to become aware that she is not able to undo the frustration of her wishes through the activity of her hand. Until that time the hand has served as a means of identifying her activity with that of her mother. When she is forced to recognize that she cannot fulfill the wish to identify her body with her mother's—as, for instance, by being able to produce a baby of her own—the activity of the hand becomes a source of anxiety for the girl. Instead of being identified with the gratifying object, the hand is now potentially identified with a depriving and frustrating one since the child no longer feels that she can satisfy her wishes through its use.

Such a view implies that the girl's continued use of masturbation beyond the oedipal phase is defensive against the underlying anxiety aroused by the impulse to reject or hate her body as a source of disappointment and frustration. The continued effort to experience the body as a source of gratification via masturbation may enable the girl to maintain a defensive idealization of her own body, but at the expense of maintaining the repression of her hostility toward the mother and denial of the disappointing reality of her own body in comparison with her mother's.

From a developmental point of view, everything we have said about the basis for the girl's relationship to her body seems equally true for the boy. The difference in the time taken by girls and boys before they turn away from exclusive attachment to the mother can be explained by the encouragement given to the girl—through her own observation of having a body similar to her mother's—to cling to the expectation of being able to identify with all her mother's activity for much longer than the boy.

Although we have suggested that the ultimate wish, which is experienced as a source of frustration for the girl, is for a body that can produce a baby and not necessarily for a body that includes a penis, we do not see this as the essential issue. A central issue of the preoedipal period is the conflict between activity and passivity and the need for the child to internalize a mother who is felt as caring actively for the child's body as a means of becoming separate from her (Brunswick 1940). In examining the significance masturbation has for the development of the child's relationship to its own body, we are concerned to show how the activity of the hand in relation to the body permits the child to feel that its own body is capable of providing a source of satisfaction independently of the mother. We are less concerned here with the actual content of the fantasy or wish. Our experience within the transference of analyzing female patients has often confirmed this view. The patient's experience of the transference is of a hostile, depriving mother who withholds that which would enable the patient to become like the analyst. The suspicion is that the analyst behaves in this way in order to keep the patient helpless and to force her to remain passively dependent on the analyst.

THE MASTURBATION CONFLICT OF THE FEMALE ADOLESCENT

The effect of puberty on the girl, according to Freud (1905, 1931), is to set in motion a renewal of the repression of masturbation. The implication is that the girl reacts to puberty as a confirmation of her lack of a penis. If the relationship to her body includes accepting that her body cannot replace totally the mother's as part of the oedipal resolution, Freud's explanation for the repression of masturbation following puberty no longer follows. Puberty now fulfills the old wish of having a body that is able to produce a child. We see the anxiety aroused at puberty as due to other factors, which once more lead to the girl's avoidance of the use of the hand in relation to her own genitals.

Inasmuch as the hand is unconsciously identified with the caring and gratifying aspects of the mother, the experience of sexual pleasure through the use of the hand will unconsciously be experienced as fulfillment of the wish to be passively gratified by the mother. But the emergence of this wish into consciousness opens the way to the active seeking of a homosexual object choice as a means of defending against passive wishes, and can potentially interfere with the choice of a male as the sexual object. Fantasies of caring for or of rescuing the mother (and, in the transference, the analyst) are evidence of the need for an active identification to defend against these passive wishes. But puberty poses a new threat for the female who continued to use masturbation during latency as a means of both maintaining an active identification with the mother and denying the reality of the inadequacy of her own body. In order to maintain this defensive struggle in relation to her body through masturbation, the girl now becomes vulnerable to being forced into making a homosexual object choice. At the same time, the identification of her pubertal body with that of her mother's makes the need to maintain the idealized relation-

ship to her own body even more urgent in order to keep repressed the hatred of her mother's sexual body and her own.

This particular aspect of puberty—the girl's having a body
which is identified with her mother's—is of crucial importance
in the future development of her relationship to her own sexual body (Ritvo 1976). It is something that is frequently given
insufficient importance when considering difficulties in female
sexual development. If the need for the renewed suppression
of masturbation following puberty is understood as avoidance
of the use of the hand for masturbatory purposes, rather than
just as the suppression of masturbation, it follows that what is
being avoided is the depriving and frustrating potential that is
unconsciously felt to be contained in the activity of the hand in
relation to the genitals, now identified with the mother's sexual
body.

Some analysts have used their clinical observations to show
that adolescent girls do masturbate and have stated that those
who consciously do not are denying their awareness of the way
in which they use other activities for masturbatory purposes.
The implication, therefore, is that there is no basic difference
between male and female adolescents in the significance of
masturbatory activity (see Clower 1975). For the boy, it is part
of his progressive move of separating and differentiating his
body from the mother's; for the girl, the same activity can instead be experienced as being forced to submit to the identification of her body with her mother's sexual body.

The nature of the anxiety aroused as a result of puberty can
be properly understood only by taking into account the meanings that masturbation can have for the adolescent girl. These
anxieties help to explain the intensity of the struggle that exists
for some adolescent girls against masturbation, which may result in the compelling need to attack their bodies actively with
their hand. The choice of the wrist or arm as the area for self-
injury can then be understood as part of the effort to control
the hand by symbolically cutting it off from the body. Our own
clinical observations suggest that the impulse for self-cutting
occurred at times when the patient experienced a fear of giving
in to the regressive wish to be passively cared for; the self-dam-

age was preceded by an outburst of uncontrolled hostility against the mother, the sexual partner, or the analyst.

CLINICAL MATERIAL

Gloria

Gloria, a young married woman, anxiously said at the start of her analysis that she hoped the analyst would not try to make her feel guilty about masturbating. Her husband knew of it, and they both felt there was nothing wrong with it. She said she would resent it very much if the analyst created a problem about it. Despite this effort to avoid feelings of resentment, she experienced the first period of her analysis as overwhelmingly frustrating and the analyst as totally depriving. After her marriage broke up, she became involved in a new heterosexual relationship and told of masturbating after feeling disappointed by sexual intercourse, with the accompanying angry thought: "Now I can do without you!" Consciously she was angry with her lover, but the person being attacked in her fantasy could clearly be understood in the transference to be related to her female analyst, representing both her mother and a sexual woman with whom she wanted to compete.

Before starting this new affair, the patient had become very anxious when the close relationship she had with a female friend had led to some physical contact. She had been both excited and frightened by the experience because it made her consciously aware of her fear that she might be sexually abnormal. This could be related to old feelings about her body, her hatred of it, and her fear that it was damaged and that she would be unable to have a child. In the analysis it could be linked to much earlier feelings and fantasies related to not having been wanted as a child by her mother and subsequently feeling that her mother wanted her to be injured and unable to have children. The regressive pull of the wish to experience the mother as gratifying, which was repeated in the analysis, was determined by the intensity of her old disappointment and anger and her fear of having to submit to the fantasied, punitive, preoedipal mother.

She had masturbated actively throughout her childhood and at times when she knew she might be discovered by her mother. In adolescence her hostile, demanding behavior was expressed in delinquent acts outside the home, while the regressive wish to be gratified by the mother was expressed in a fantasy that her mother was forcing her to offer herself sexually to a man in return for money, which she would then have to give to her mother. This fantasy expressed her wish to feel that her mother was responsible for her sexual activity and that her desire was not to destroy her mother but instead to help her live. The fantasy was repeated during her analysis in a dream Gloria had one night after having masturbated. She dreamed that the analyst was suggesting that she go to work. Although the impulse to masturbate was related to feelings of frustration in an ongoing heterosexual relationship, the fantasy that had to be denied was the homosexual one of being gratified by the mother or the female analyst, which she needed in order to defend against the anxiety of wanting to attack her own body as the source of the frustration.

Selma

A similar fantasy was reported by Selma, an older married patient. She had always worried that she was sexually abnormal because the only way she could become sexually aroused by her husband was through the creation of a fantasy while she was having intercourse: A repulsive old woman watched her being forcibly raped by a man and scolded her for resisting him while encouraging the man to humiliate her even more. Only in this way could she allow herself to enjoy intercourse, through the fantasy of giving in to the wish to be cared for by her mother. Yet at the same time by needing to use this fantasy, she felt that she was proving herself to be abnormal.

This patient brought no memories of having masturbated as a child. But she remembered with a great deal of guilt that she had had such violent fights with a younger brother that her mother was afraid of leaving her alone with him. She also recalled that her mother used to beat her as a child.

Her sexual fantasy could be understood as a wish that her mother, represented by the repulsive woman in the fantasy, was still in control of her body because sexual excitement for her was identified with uncontrollable violence against her mother's babies. Her hatred of her own body for containing this violence was expressed in the transference by her feeling that her female analyst must be disgusted by her sexual fantasies, hated her, and therefore also hated her body. The woman in her fantasy was old and repulsive to defend against recognizing her wish for a young, attractive woman to caress and who would want her body. In this way Selma could feel free of her own hatred of her body and of the need to hurt and attack herself as she felt she did in intercourse by having such a fantasy. During her adolescence she had also become frightened when a close relationship to a girl threatened to develop into a homosexual one. In the transference the renewal of this wish could be seen in her demand that the analyst should love her body and caress her because she felt this was the only way she could undo her own hatred of her body. Not doing so, she felt, was proof of the analyst's disgust for her.

This case shows how the actual experience of being beaten by her mother had become part of the patient's own masochistic relationship to her body and was represented in her fantasy by feeling forced to put her body in the position of being humiliated and hurt by a man. As a child, while she avoided touching herself, her fear of what her own hand would do to her body if she did touch herself by masturbating was expressed in violent attacks on her brother. After puberty Selma's wish for the loving, caring hand of another woman to touch her and thus make her body feel lovable became the only way she felt she could control the violence she was afraid she might direct against herself.

Harriet

After an initial interview, Harriet, a married woman, told of a dream where the female analyst was identified with a woman with whom, in reality, she had felt uncomfortable. She had suspected this woman of homosexual tendencies because of the way the woman would touch her every time they met. In her analysis she talked of waking up at night to find her hand touching her genitals. This made her feel terribly anxious and ashamed lest she might have masturbated in her sleep. She could relieve her anxiety only by trying to urinate. If she was able to do so, this indicated that she had been awakened only by the need to urinate and not because she had been secretly masturbating.

Harriet had had a lonely, isolated childhood with no memories of any pleasurable experiences shared with her mother. Her first anxiety attack had occurred in early adolescence during her first prolonged absence from home. She had found it extremely difficult to urinate and was convinced that she would have to return home because she believed she needed the presence of her mother to urinate.

Her anxiety about needing to urinate was related to the fantasy that her mother had deprived her as a child of a strong body, which would have enabled her to feel brave, like a man, instead of anxious, like her mother, a woman. The identification of her hand with the deprivation she felt she had experienced from her mother made her consciously terrified of touching her husband's or her children's genitals.

At adolescence the need for her mother to be present so that she could urinate represented a breakthrough into consciousness of the masturbatory meaning urination had for her. The wish was to experience her need to urinate as still being her mother's responsibility and an activity they could share. Only in this way could she feel that her wish to attack her mother's body could remain controlled. Later it was learned that if she urinated in strange toilets, she always did so standing up because of her fear of contamination. Therefore her fear that she would have to return home to her mother also expressed her need to give in to her mother to maintain her fantasy of being able to be like a boy.

These clinical examples show that the need to suppress the masturbatory activity of the hand during adolescence is closely linked both to the fear of bringing into consciousness the passive homosexual wishes in relation to the mother and also to the anxiety aroused as the result of experiencing the body as now having the potential of living out the destructive retaliatory wishes directed against the mother's body. Further clinical material illustrates this more clearly. Each of the patients had formed an intense relationship either with another girl or with an adult woman during midadolescence. From the patients' accounts and the reconstructions of the meaning within the analysis, these relationships had symbolically represented the living out of mutually gratifying and exciting masturbatory activity—something that is part of the normal development of the young adolescent. Significantly, each of these patients had broken off these relationships precipitously when some external event had made the patient feel that the other girl had been harmed or had suffered as the result of their shared activity. This may be taken as evidence that the conflict that leads to the avoidance of the use of the hand in masturbation for the adolescent girl is related to the anxiety aroused by experiencing her body as capable of destructiveness. Such an explanation makes it possible to understand the tendency seen in many seriously disturbed adolescent girls to behavior that aims at controlling their bodies through self-inflicted physical damage.

THE FEMALE OEDIPUS COMPLEX, PREGNANCY, AND MOTHERHOOD IN ADOLESCENCE

In giving up masturbation as part of the integration of her relationship to her body at the phallic phase, the girl "accepts" the reality of her body's incapacity to fulfill her wish to produce a baby. Accepting this reality means not being allowed to identify herself and her body with that of the active, powerful mother who can both gratify and frustrate. Her continued dependence on the mother for gratification of her needs forces her to submit to a mother whom she now experiences as envious and frustrating. The extent to which the girl feels this as a threat and a denial of her right to take over an active role determines how much she will need to seek reassurance through identification with the father's active role in his relationship to the mother. Her wish, in identification with her father, is to have a body that can be used like his to give her mother a baby (Brunswick 1940) and so to free herself from her hatred of her mother for not allowing her to have a body that can make a baby. At the same time, she can use such an identification with the father defensively against the anxiety of feeling forced to submit passively to the active, phallic mother—a process similar to the one used by the boy.

"Activity" becomes at this period a male quality, one that the girl feels she needs to possess. She is envious of the male for possessing this quality, while also having defensively to devalue the mother's active role. The possession of a penis and her own pleasurable clitoral sensations become inextricably linked in fantasy with activity and with the father's active role in relation to the mother.

Earlier in this chapter, we described how the girl's continued use of masturbation beyond the phallic-oedipal period is determined by anxiety and by the need to continue to experience the body as capable of providing satisfaction in order to keep repressed the hatred and fear of the mother. The fantasy accompanying masturbation can now begin to contain an identification of her body with her father's as a further defensive measure against the hatred of the mother. This identification forms the basis, following puberty, of the adolescent girl's fear that her body is damaged and will be incapable of producing a child. The damage is unconsciously felt to be the result of her own activity and the pleasure she derived from it. This fear may be so extreme in the young adolescent that it can lead to a compelling need to become pregnant before she has been able to establish a stable heterosexual object relationship. A baby is felt to be the only means through which she can undo her emptiness and the fear of now being alone with her damaged body. But in becoming a mother herself she is unconsciously giving up her relationship to her body as a source of active pleasure; instead, she is submitting passively to the mother.

The opposition that continues to exist for all adolescent girls between the need for pleasurable experiences from the body and the fear of being forced to submit to the internalized mother who is seen as envious and frustrating, also makes the late adolescent and young woman afraid that, in fulfilling her normal wish for a baby, she must now renounce the possibility of pleasure and activity. The earlier anxiety about being forced into passive dependence on her mother turns into the fantasy that, in now being able to fulfill her wish to have a baby, she will be "castrated" and frustrated in her own active search for pleasure. The unconscious fear of needing to choose between pleasure and motherhood also can find expression in a conflict between giving up masturbation and a sexual relationship with a man. The girl who has previously masturbated during adolescence may experience the sexual relationship as disappointing—feeling that only she can give herself pleasure. Unconsciously she is unable to choose to surrender her body to a man because of the fantasy that, in allowing penetration, she is now finally submitting to the frustrating and damaging mother.

For some women, the pleasure they experience in the sexual relationship remains based exclusively on the identification of their vagina with a maternally active role toward the man's penis (Deutsch 1932, 1945). It is as if the vagina can only become integrated safely as part of the new sexual body on condition that the active search for pleasure through orgasmic experience is renounced.

The adolescent girl who chooses to abort a pregnancy may often become involved in a repetitive search for reassurance that her body is not damaged. In rejecting the child she feels as if she has rejected femininity; her unconscious fear of her body being damaged becomes intensified as a result of the abortion. This can often result in a renewed need to become pregnant. For those adolescents who keep the baby, the danger is that the baby can then take over the role of denying her the right for activity and satisfaction of her own needs. The young mother may then feel compelled to punish or attack the baby instead of attacking her own body.

The final integration of the sexually mature genitals for the adolescent girl revolves around the ability to differentiate between the uterus—that can safely grow a baby—and the vagina—that can be used in her relationship to a man. In the seriously disturbed adolescent girl the final differentiation between the uterus and the vagina cannot take place. The vagina continues to be experienced as containing her hatred while the capacity for bearing a child remains unintegrated as part of her relationship to her own body.

5
The Superego, the Idealized Body Image, and Puberty

The superego plays a crucial role in determining the success or failure of the adolescent's move toward establishing the final sexual organization. Many of the problems that may arise during adolescence result from the inability of the superego to allow for a change in the earlier identifications and in the quality of its demands on the ego, despite the pressure to do so following physical sexual maturity.

Anna Freud (1937), in a chapter entitled "Instinctual Anxiety During Puberty," says, "In so far as the superego is at this period still cathected with libido derived from the relation to the parents, it is itself treated as a suspicious incestuous object. . . . The ego *alienates* itself from the superego also. To young people this *partial repression* of the superego, the estrangement from part of its contents, is one of the greatest troubles of adolescence. The principal effect of the rupture . . . is to increase the danger which threatens from the instincts" (p. 182, italics added). This view is widely understood to mean that the adolescent's tendency toward certain forms of compulsive activity—delinquency, aggressive or sexual behavior—results from this temporary lack of a superego to control his behavior, because of the need to detach himself from the oedipal objects and their internalized representative. Jacobson (1964) also describes "the disruption" that takes place in the relationship of the ego to the superego during adolescence. She describes how a gradual restructuring of the ego has to occur and how a new ego ideal structure has to be formed to create an "effective bridge" once more between the ego and the superego.

In this chapter we examine how partial repression of the superego affects the vulnerable adolescent. The inability to create the effective bridge postulated by Jacobson may bring about vulnerability to later pathological development for these adolescents. We will show how these adolescents are unable to detach themselves temporarily or partially from the demands of the superego but continue to remain dependent on it throughout the developmental period. The superego's demands allow them no respite from the pressure it exerts.

The physical changes that begin at puberty have a temporary destabilizing effect on the narcissistic equilibrium that existed during latency. For the vulnerable adolescent, puberty is experienced as a potentially traumatic event. His anxiety in relation to the bodily changes necessitates constant defensive measures to maintain the narcissistic cathexis of the body and to deal with the anxiety that is felt as threatening. The new danger is of experiencing hatred for the sexual body because of the temporary lack of libidinal investment of the body following puberty.

To understand why such continued dependence on the superego may exist during adolescence, we examine its role in maintaining the narcissistic equilibrium (the libidinal investment of his body and of himself) under three headings:

1. masturbation and the idealized body image;
2. the ego ideal and the move to new object relationships; and
3. the use of the transference relationship by the ill adolescent.

Masturbation and the Idealized Body Image The conflict surrounding masturbation during adolescence normally derives its intensity from the superego's opposition to allowing into consciousness the revived oedipal wishes through the fantasies accompanying masturbation. This stands in the way of the adolescent's efforts to use masturbation as a means of taking over the ownership of his newly matured sexual body. Ownership of the sexual body means that the adolescent assumes responsibility for his sexual wishes and the new aggressive potential; it also means giving up the relationship to the oedipal objects, which existed during latency and was based on his prepubertal body. This loss of the old relationship constitutes the change in the narcissistic cathexis of the body that occurs as a result of the pubertal changes; the loss cannot be undone through the relationship to the mother. Instead, the adolescent is left temporarily feeling alone and vulnerable and hating his sexual body, which is blamed for the narcissistic injury.

The child's development from the time of birth to the end of the oedipal period represents a continuous separation of his own body from the mother's (Dibble and Cohen 1981; Mahler, Pine, and Bergman 1975; Winnicott 1953). This begins with internalization of the differentiation of self and object representations and is followed by separation from the mother's care of his body. Each phase of such separation is accompanied by a loss of direct libidinal gratification from the mother and a building up of an internalized body image that eventually includes the child's genitals. Only later, following puberty, does another change in the body image include the identification of the body with that of the oedipal parent and his or her power to procreate. For progressive development and separation to continue, the child has to find a means of dealing with the anxiety related to the loss of the experience of gratification of his libidinal needs by the mother. This can be conceptualized as taking the form of an idealized body image that is created in fantasy and becomes internalized at each stage of development alongside the actual body image. Such a fantasy of the idealized body image enables the child to feel that his body still contains the potential for restoring the blissful state of omnipotent fusion with the mother (Lewin 1950) despite the actual separation that is taking place. The pubertal body changes initiate a new and decisive phase of separation from the mother's body and from her physical care. The new sexual body in terms of the oedipal identifications means that the narcissistic investment of that image can no longer be dependent on the mother's physical care. Instead, the adolescent has to be able to depend on his own activity—either autoerotically or by involving a nonincestuous object—for the renewal of the narcissistic investment of his body to include the mature genital body.

For those adolescents who were able to maintain their narcissistic equilibrium throughout latency only by excessive dependence on the idealized body image as an internal source of reassurance, puberty revives intense anxiety and a wish to deny the bodily changes taking place. Masturbation may have been used by the latency child as a way of experiencing himself in fantasy as the idealized child united with his mother, but it now takes on a new meaning. Instead of acting as a source of reassurance, masturbation increases the anxiety. Instead of being able to use it as a trial action for genital activity in fantasy, the adolescent is forced by his anxiety to use it to continue to live out passive preoedipal fantasies. This maintains the fantasied, prepubertal, idealized body image and protects his new sexual body from the hatred that can now be directed against it. This renewed dependence on the preoedipal, idealized body image means that masturbation therefore cannot be used to integrate the new sexual body as a source for new gratification. Instead, masturbation is experienced passively as something the adolescent feels compelled to do. The sexual body is a persecutor, and the preoedipal body is the only one that has a potential for making the adolescent feel safe.

These are the adolescents who are vulnerable. Their inability to allow for a change in the body image means that instead of continued progressive development, developmental breakdown occurs. Clinically this can be observed in those adolescents who feel compelled to include fetishistic objects or rituals as part of their masturbatory activity or whose main interest is directed toward erotogenic zones other than the genitals, such as the mouth, anus, or skin. Their continued dependence on feeling able to maintain the union in fantasy with the omnipotent mother (through the use of the fantasy of the idealized body image) means that by the end of adolescence the idealized, prepubertal body image becomes integrated as a part of the final sexual organization. This will determine their sexual functioning in adulthood without any change in the quality of the demands of the superego.

Even when dependence on maintaining the preoedipal body image is not so extreme, the anxiety surrounding masturbation may still be intense because the adolescent consciously feels alone with his new sexual body. The resulting sexual behavior may be determined more by the need to find a nonincestuous object with whom to share the experience of the new sexual body than by the need to deny the change that is taking place in the body. Sexual activity with a partner then has to take over the function normally fulfilled by masturbation. It has to be used primarily as a means of establishing the narcissistic cathexis of the young adolescent's sexual body. The conflict that is then experienced is related to denial of the existence or the value of genitals other than the adolescent's own.

We have seen a number of older adolescent girls who were worried about not being able to have a stable heterosexual relationship. Often we learned that heterosexual activity began soon after puberty and then took on a compelling quality, sometimes in sexual relationships that were soon broken off, only to be renewed with another partner. During treatment it became clear that these girls were frightened of sexual intercourse and unconsciously felt it was an attack on their bodies to which they had to submit. Intercourse represents the danger that the male's possession of a penis contains the power to destroy the girl's own fantasy of having an undefined and undifferentiated sexual organ rather than a vagina. Unconsciously she experiences her body as still being able to fulfill both roles of phallic and castrated—that is, not differentiated as female. Such an idealized body image (of having both a phallic and a castrated body) may be needed by the adolescent who is developing normally as a means of defending against the anxiety of a loss of narcissistic cathexis of the body image.

But what can be observed clinically as an interference in development is the need to cling to this new, fantasied body image instead of the adolescent having it available as a temporary means to create an effective bridge (Jacobson 1964) toward full male or female differentiation by the end of adolescence. Instead, their adult sexual functioning will continue to be interfered with by the dependence on this fantasy. For more severely disturbed adolescents who remain totally dependent on the preoedipal, idealized body image, the risk of a break with external reality during adolescence can become a real one.

Their dependence on maintaining the idealized body image through masturbation and their inability to allow for any compromise solution can cause the actual bodily changes to be perceived as delusional or to be projected into persecutory experiences that appear to come from the outside world instead of from themselves. The withdrawal this compels them to effect from the objects in the external world can then result in total dependence on physical care from the real oedipal objects as the only way in which such adolescents can continue to function.

The idealized body image does not have to contain the actual fantasy of a reunion with the mother's body—that is, of a return to the undifferentiated state of fusion with the idealized omnipotent mother. The experience of gratification contains the fantasy of union with the mother via the idealized body image, which has been developed during the preoedipal period.

The Ego Ideal and the Move to New Object Relationships We can refer to the ego ideal only when it has become one of the functions of the superego—that is, after the dissolution of the oedipus complex and the formation of the superego into a cohesive structure. The content of the ego ideal therefore becomes fixed at a time when the child is still dependent on the parents and where a component of the ego ideal is related to acceptance of this reality. The extent to which the adolescent continues to be dependent on the need to fulfill the expectations of the ego ideal in order to feel secure and loved can act as an interference with progressive development. The extent to which he conforms to the expectations of the ego ideal is a measure of the degree to which he has had to renounce the active seeking of gratification in order to feel secure in the face of his anxiety. What has become internalized is a dependence on maintaining a *passive* role in relation to the domination of the superego. In order for the adolescent to feel free to change the relationship to the superego and to take over an *active* role in relation to his new sexual body, he must free himself from the restrictions imposed on his sexual activity by the superego with the expectations of the ego ideal.

Following puberty, object relationships made outside the family, especially with peers, take on a new meaning in relation to this task. By identifying with the expectations he feels are coming from his peers, the adolescent now thinks he has a "new" ego ideal on which he can depend for his narcissistic supplies. The role of these new identifications in helping progressive development to take place is fully acknowledged in the literature on normal adolescent development. However, the vulnerable adolescent, as described earlier, is so dependent on the superego for approval that he cannot risk effecting even a temporary or partial repression of its demands in favor of the new demands created through identifications with his peers. He then loses the opportunity for identifying with their so-called demand to take over an active sexual role, and the adolescent remains dependent on the superego and on identification with ideals that demand the acceptance of a passive sexual role in order to feel loved.

We then may see the use of a "pseudo ego ideal" (M. Laufer 1964), an ideal which represents the adolescent's attempt to deny the extent to which he still feels dependent on fulfilling the demands of the oedipal ego ideal to ensure a source of feeling loved. Such a pseudo ego ideal may take the form of trying to deny the shame that is attached to wanting to be a good, obedient, clean child by identifying with peers who represent the opposite. The vulnerable adolescent may try to use as an ego ideal a relationship to a fantasy object, which demands control of the sexual body. We have in mind the ideal of asceticism, various forms of body control such as fasting, or self-punishment as a means of maintaining an internal source of approval; at the same time such forms of behavior betray the adolescent's vulnerability by the attack they represent on his sexual body and by their defensive function.

Independently of the extent to which integration of the new sexual body image has been able to proceed, these adolescents remain unable to change the image of themselves from that of a dependent child to that of an active, potent adult (Blos 1972). For the boy, the necessary aggressive aspect of adult sexual functioning may be felt as creating an impossible barrier to establishing sexual relationships, while for the girl the normal passive aspect of her sexual functioning may become intensified to a degree that makes her feel that she is not in charge of or responsible for her choice—as if she has to remain totally dependent on the object to avoid feeling blamed (Ritvo 1976). Even though it appears as if they are able to make nonincestuous, heterosexual relationships, unconsciously they remain tied to the oedipal parent through the relationship to the superego and the need to live up to its expectations.

The Use of the Transference Relationship by the Ill Adolescent Our descriptions of the role played by the superego in preventing progressive development, addressed in the preceding sections, are derived from our observations of the use of the transference by vulnerable adolescents. These observations led us to question the assumptions used to explain the difficulties that arise when using classical analytic technique in the treatment of the ill adolescent. The traditional explanation of these difficulties has been that, since a partial repression of the superego *must* take place for development to proceed normally, the transference relationship in adolescence represents a hindrance to normal development because it fosters the creation of a regressive libidinal tie to the analyst. Our experience is that the ill adolescent is unable to effect such a detachment from the oedipal objects represented within the superego. It is just this continued dependence that interferes in his move toward normal adulthood. The dependence on the analyst, far from being a hindrance to the ill adolescent's development, contains and repeats the conflicts that result from this dependence and provides the only means through which he can begin to risk giving up his dependence on maintaining the pre-oedipal idealized body image and the passive aspects of the oedipal ego ideal. We see the analyst enabling the effective bridge to be created.

Jacobson (1964) describes the difficulties of the severely disturbed adolescent as resulting from defensive operations that are necessitated "by the transitory collapse of the superego and the *repressive barrier*" (italics added). Although we agree that a transitory collapse has occurred, we do not think that the superego function lost to the ill adolescent through this collapse is that of the repressive barrier. As stated earlier, this is more relevant in the case of the normal or less disturbed adolescent who is experiencing conflict but is still able to detach himself from the oedipal objects and move toward adulthood. From our clinical observations we think the transitory collapse that occurs for the ill adolescent is in the area of the adolescent's ability to care for his own body. The defensive struggles that result are related to dealing with the regressive pull toward pregenital functioning to which the ill adolescent is exposed because of this collapse.

We have found that the regressive features characteristic of the severely disturbed adolescent, which betray their pathological nature by the use of primitive defense mechanisms of splitting and projection, act primarily as expressions of the adolescent's hatred of his own sexual body. We have described in some of the clinical examples how the analyst has to take over a caring function with the adolescent who is at risk. By risk we mean behavior such as attempted suicide, drug taking, and anorexia, but we also have in mind attacks directed specifically at the sexual body and the destruction of the adolescent's normal heterosexual functioning. We have found that the classical transference situation allows the ill adolescent to experience the analyst as temporarily taking over the caring function of his body, so that he can then begin to try giving up his dependence on regressive means of gratification. This experience of the transference has made us define the "temporary collapse" that occurs at puberty in terms of the narcissistic investment of the body and relate the self-destructive aspects of the ill adolescent's functioning to the collapse of his ability to care for his body after it takes on a new sexual significance.

The caring function of the superego was originally subsumed under Freud's concept of the "self-preservative instinct" (1920), which we felt repeatedly was lacking in the ill adolescent and which convinced us that we had to stand in the way of the adolescent's disregard of the reality dangers to which he was compelled to expose himself. The caring aspect of the superego arises developmentally from the identification and internalization of the protective aspects of parental caring (Ritvo and Solnit 1958) and, insofar as the child feels himself worthy of being cared for, it enables him to act in a caring and protective manner toward himself (Beres and Obers 1950; Loewald 1979; Sandler 1960; Schafer 1960).

At adolescence, the destabilizing effect of puberty on the narcissistic cathexis of the new sexual body leaves the adolescent vulnerable to feeling that his body does not deserve to be cared for. It is as if he cannot protect it from the aggression or hatred that is still directed at it via the superego condemnation of his sexuality. Far from being able to repress the demands of the superego, he becomes even more dependent on it as the only means of replacing the narcissistic cathexis he feels he has lost. The compelling quality that is always a characteristic of self-destructive behavior is therefore not a result of the collapse of the repressive barrier but is determined by the anxiety the adolescent experiences in feeling that he can no longer depend on himself to care for his own body.

This view of the use of the transference by the ill adolescent also enables us to understand a specific countertransference reaction. We have often been aware of feeling that the adolescent was using the analyst to live out his regressive fantasies rather than analyze them, and that there seemed to be a danger of the analyst's becoming involved in a relationship that gratified the regressive needs of the adolescent. However, we are beginning to understand such unconscious collusion by the analyst as the means through which the adolescent feels himself being cared for. The analysis, in becoming a vehicle for living out the regressive sexual fantasies, enables the ill adolescent, through identification with the analyst's care, to feel that he does not need to reject or attack his body. Technically this places a special burden on the analyst's ability to maintain a caring attitude that the adolescent can experience as being related to his body and progressive development. It demands of the analyst the ability to make conscious the adolescent's sexual wishes as expressed in his transference behavior, so that the adolescent can feel that the analyst can help him remain in control. The analyst must also be able to deal with the adolescent's hatred resulting from the continued frustration of these wishes through the analyst's demand that he put understanding in the place of gratification. In this sense the analyst's role of standing in the way of compelling self-destructive behavior outside the analytic situation allows the adolescent to experience his sexual body as cared for by the analyst (even though it will also contain some gratification of his more regressive wishes). It is as if the analyst can act as a temporary replacement of the caring function of the superego and allow the adolescent to experience his destructive hatred of the internalized, prohibiting oedipal parents in the transference instead of needing to direct it at his own body. Through experiencing and understanding his own self-hatred within the transference, the ill adolescent becomes more able to detach himself from submission to the superego because of his dependence on the ego-ideal function of the superego for his narcissistic supply as a means of replacing the lost narcissistic cathexis of his body.

The defensive use made of the transference as a means of unconsciously experiencing gratification can remain helpful in protecting the adolescent only so long as the analyst appears to be in control of the situation. When the behavior does not appear to yield to any insight and loses none of its compelling quality despite verbalization, a situation may arise where the adolescent feels that the analyst is not able to control the adolescent's behavior. What can then develop is a paranoid transference in which the analyst is experienced as the source of the adolescent's own passive sexual wishes, and the hatred then becomes directed at the analyst. The adolescent's anxiety may become overwhelming because of the need to punish and attack the analyst instead of himself. The development of such a paranoid transference can lead to the adolescent breaking off the analytic relationship as a way of ridding himself of the analyst, who has now become identified with his own forbidden, active sexual wishes and whom he feels he can no longer keep safe from his wish to attack the analyst.

Freud (1924) stresses the role of the superego in determining whether "the ego remains true to its dependence on the external world and attempts to silence the id" (neurosis) or "whether it lets itself be overcome by the id and thus torn away from reality" (psychosis) (p. 151). He describes the alternative to these two outcomes as the situation in which "the ego deforms itself by submitting to encroachments on its own unity and even perhaps by effecting a cleavage or division of itself" (fetishism) (p. 152–153). In stressing the role played by the superego in determining the direction taken by mental disturbances in adulthood, Freud also offers a model for understanding why, during adolescence, we can first begin to see the direction of the person's future mental functioning. At puberty the relationship of the superego to the ego becomes disrupted and then has to find a means of reestablishing that relationship to include a sexual identity acceptable to the superego. The ill adolescent's lack of means for achieving such a change is due to a failure to establish a positive relationship to his own sexual body without, as Freud says, "the ego deforming itself" and perhaps effecting a "cleavage or division of itself." One area where the ego may be forced to deform itself is in the internalization of a distorted body image—that is, one that represents a compromise between the preoedipal, idealized body image and the reality of the sexual body.

II
BREAKDOWN AND
THE TREATMENT PROCESS

6
Breakdown, Transference, and Reconstruction

We can assume that the adolescent who is sufficiently concerned about himself to acknowledge that he needs therapeutic help is unconsciously aware of being out of touch with part of his internal life; he feels he does not have the choice to do what he wants with his life. The reality of a physically mature body confronts him with the fact, albeit also unconsciously, that his fantasies now contain a new dimension—namely, that he is a sexual being and that his past solutions to conflict now hinder his development. In the past he may have been able to explain away his behavior, feelings, and fantasies, but after puberty he is for the first time in his life faced with the realization that past solutions to present conflicts may mean abnormal development, especially in relation to sexual life and object relationships. When he talks of his internal life, he is telling us that he feels as if he now has a passive relationship to his body and to a part of his fantasy life that forces itself upon him and, perhaps more importantly, forces him to feel and behave in ways that are out of his control. An adolescent patient who says, for example, that she hates herself because she feels compelled to eat or feels like ripping out her insides so that she can stop masturbating may be describing the content of her central masturbation fantasy, but emotionally she feels that there is nothing inside her to help her deal with the repetitive onslaught from her body. For her, her sexual body is not only an enemy but the representative of her abnormality.

We have used the word "unconsciously" when referring to

the adolescent's feeling or awareness about himself because to put the adolescent in touch with what he feels or may know takes a good deal of time in treatment, but when it happens he conveys, often with relief, that he is familiar with his hopelessness or with his sense of being out of control or with his awareness that something has been seriously wrong for some time.

By the time the adolescent comes to treatment, his distorted sexual body image has already been integrated into the ego to some extent, and this will express itself in his present object relationships. We may see anything from a total absence of sexual relationships to those that contain obvious elements of perverse development. The extent of this integration varies a great deal depending on the quality of the gratification the patient obtains from his central masturbation fantasy, the severity of the regression that has taken place, and the extent to which his function of reality testing is intact. The presence of pathology in adolescence always means that there is a disturbance in relation to the person's sexual life, and the understanding of this disturbance is fundamental to the therapeutic task.

The adolescent will not say "there is something wrong with my sexual body" but may instead complain of loneliness, isolation, the feeling that relationships never have the meaning he seeks. But anxiety about his distorted sexual body image and his failure to alter it is expressed through his feelings about these relationships. Whatever else may seem wrong to the adolescent, he is unconsciously aware that he is failing as a sexual being. His superego never lets him forget this even though he may have available a wide range of ways that help him deny his failure.

In 1906, Freud put forward the view that fantasies (or imaginary memories), mostly produced during puberty, may be inserted between symptoms and childish impressions and can then be transformed more directly into symptoms (p. 274). One of Freud's purposes was to question his earlier views about childhood experiences and to suggest a revised view about the nature of hysterical fantasies; nevertheless, his statement about fantasies during puberty is directly relevant to what we wish to say about the treatment process during adolescence as well as about the relationship between therapeutic intervention in ado-

lescence and the prevention of organized pathology after adolescence. We place importance on Freud's statement because of
the implication that certain fantasies in adolescence can become
integrated into a pathological sexual organization and that this
integration is much less reversible after adolescence. It also implies that treatment can have a preventive function, inasmuch
as it may enable the adolescent to feel that he has an active
choice in either integrating or rejecting these fantasies as part
of his sexual organization rather than being forced to give in
passively to their power and potentially symptomatic outcome.

In this chapter, we concentrate on those therapeutic issues
that we consider essential to undoing the effect of breakdown
in adolescence and removing the pathological factors that
would otherwise result in an abnormal outcome by the end of
adolescence and in adulthood. These issues are specific to the
adolescent patient in that they are tied to the nature of adolescent pathology and its effect on the person's future sexual and
work life. We can summarize them as follows:

1. *The therapeutic process* must ultimately make conscious the
   presence of a distorted body image and the adolescent's
   wish for the therapist to participate in or accept this distortion, including the distortion of external reality that this implies;
2. *The breakdown* that took place at puberty must be reexperienced within the transference relationship. A "transference
   breakdown" must be established and worked through.[1]

THE THERAPEUTIC PROCESS

Only within the safety of the transference relationship can the
adolescent's pathology begin to take on emotional meaning,
which includes a sense of the historical development of his
present ways of functioning. Possibly of greater importance,

---

1. We have described adolescent pathology as constituting a breakdown in
the developmental process rather than as a neurosis or psychosis. In this sense,
the term *transference neurosis* is not strictly applicable; instead, we have adopted
the term *transference breakdown*. But in using this term, we are describing a process whereby the patient's pathology becomes concentrated totally within the
analysis and in the relationship to the analyst (Freud 1914; Loewald 1971).

the transference can make emotionally real the fact that ultimately the patient can find a new way of integrating his sexual
body and his earlier incestuous wishes into a sexual identity
that does not have to contain the regressive pull of wishing to
give in. By understanding the superego strictures and infantile
ideals and by connecting them with his current sexual wishes
and fears, the adolescent patient is enabled to take charge of
his sexual body in a way that does not have to contain the repeated need and wish to give the body to the mother who first
cared for it. This is expressed in the transference by the adolescent's efforts to force the analyst to accept the distortions of his
body image and of his relation to the external world.

Through treatment the adolescent begins to see that his demands and his emotions also contain his anxiety about his sexual body. Before treatment, he never doubted his distortions of
reality and their relation to his image of himself as a sexual
person. These projections, which had been used as a defense,
strengthened his belief that he was not in charge or in control
of what he did, felt, or thought.

The therapeutic process and the transference experience not
only enable the adolescent to begin to doubt his earlier solutions but offer him new hope, making it possible for him to feel
that he is no longer alone with his pathology and shame. Perhaps for the first time in his life, he can now risk feeling the
destructiveness and hatred toward his own body and toward
the oedipal parents whom he has, until now, blamed for his pathology. The experience of the transference is an essential part
of treatment and is fundamental in helping the adolescent
scrutinize the breakdown that took place at puberty. Transference gives the adolescent and the therapist potential freedom
to acknowledge the presence and the power of the frightening
distortions, the self-hatred, the regressive or perverse fantasies,
and the original hopelessness or passive submission to the
pathology.

REEXPERIENCING THE BREAKDOWN IN THE TRANSFERENCE

In the treatment of the adolescent patient the developmental
breakdown that took place at puberty has to be reexperienced

with the analyst. This means that the content as well as the defensive maneuvers employed to deal with the sexual body and the direct sexual wishes become totally, even if only temporarily, focused on the relationship to the analyst. Unless this happens in treatment, the destructive force of the developmental breakdown does not diminish throughout adolescence (Dewald 1978; M. Laufer 1978; Ritvo 1978).

The transference and the reexperiencing of the breakdown in the transference (the transference breakdown) must be understood both historically and dynamically, as shown by the content of the central masturbation fantasy; and developmentally, as shown in the adolescent's current relationship to his sexual body—that is, to the way in which the sexual body is used or experienced in both genital and oedipal terms. From our analytic work with adolescent patients, the transference breakdown is expressed in the adolescent's unconscious need to force the analyst to participate in his sexual pathology—by trying to get the analyst to take charge of the adolescent's actions and fantasies, by demanding that the analyst seduce the adolescent sexually, or by presenting himself as sexually and socially ineffectual. Dynamically, the motivation seems to come from the adolescent patient's need to destroy his own sexual body and to offer the nonincestuous body to the mother—that is, to the person he had up to now blamed for his pathology. If the adolescent should succeed in this attempt, a relationship to the preoedipal mother would be perpetuated, and at the same time the identification with the oedipal parent of the same sex would be destroyed, resulting in a much greater distortion of his reality and his sexual life.

The seemingly insurmountable clinical problems that are often encountered in the treatment of the ill adolescent may represent avoidance to some extent, either by the patient or by the analyst, of recognizing or understanding the nature of the developmental breakdown that took place at puberty and its effect on the adolescent's present life. We may miss the meaning of this developmental breakdown to the adolescent if we understand that clinical material solely in historical terms. The same may happen if we view it primarily in terms of narcissism or prepubertal experiences. Instead, we have found it more useful to see illness during adolescence as always representing some abnormality in sexual development and functioning. Understanding this disturbance is fundamental to the analytical task.

When we refer to reexperiencing the developmental breakdown within the transference, we mean experiencing the projections, distortions, and emotions that have been tied to the sexual body and to the oedipal parents, which resulted in a temporary break with reality at puberty. By acknowledging his compulsion to live out certain fantasies (his central masturbation fantasy), the adolescent can see the connection between his present pathology and his past solutions to conflict. Making the developmental breakdown emotionally real and less traumatic enables the adolescent to understand why a breakdown took place at puberty and why it took the form it did. In this way he can begin to understand the meaning of the pathological relationship to his sexual body and the reasons for his need to distort his past and present reality in the way he has.

RECONSTRUCTION

We have not set out to discuss here the technical problems encountered during the treatment of the adolescent who has experienced a developmental breakdown. But we include remarks on reconstruction because of its relation to some of the issues raised earlier, especially the link between the adolescent's present life and pathology and his past development.

Clearly, the primary function of reconstruction is to put the adolescent in touch with the experience of the breakdown and the accompanying emotions (Freud 1937; Greenacre 1975). Unless this is accomplished, the power of the trauma of the breakdown continues to operate, and whatever else treatment may achieve, it cannot help the adolescent undo the immediate past or integrate the experience of the breakdown. The transference breakdown may take a long time to establish, but the completely safe and predictable relationship to the analyst is an essential component of the process. For the adolescent the transference breakdown means experiencing emotions and fantasies that will undoubtedly make the treatment extremely difficult both for him and for the analyst. But it is essential to keep these emotions and fantasies within the treatment and focused on the person of the analyst until their meaning in the present is understood. Although understanding the relation of the breakdown to past development is a necessary part of treatment, reconstruction may be used unintentionally by the analyst as a way of lessening the intensity of the transference experience, with the result that an important part of the treatment experience has been lost.

During the treatment there is no purpose in piecing together fantasies and experiences of the oedipal or preoedipal past while the adolescent is experiencing sexual fantasies that make no sense to him and while the breakdown that took place at puberty is still experienced as a traumatic event. The danger in treatment is that we may reconstruct the wrong thing at the wrong time, while possibly ignoring what the adolescent is telling us or is perhaps unable to tell us but wants us to know about and help him understand. We may make the mistake of assuming that "earlier" or "deeper" is necessarily better and more therapeutic. Our concentration on the wrong things and our reconstruction of the wrong "past" may be additional reasons why so many adolescents who are urgently in need of help run away from treatment.

In our treatment of adolescent patients it helps us to think of them as having "two pasts"—the more immediate past, which contains the traumatic experience at puberty, and the preadolescent past, which includes the preoedipal history, the oedipal resolutions, and the experiences of latency. Both pasts need understanding and reconstruction, but unless the immediate past makes sense to the adolescent patient, the reconstruction of the preadolescent past is a purely intellectual and emotionally dead experience.

We do not want to give the impression that we must avoid the attempt to understand the preadolescent past until we have reconstructed and helped the adolescent to work through the breakdown at puberty. We mean, rather, that we must keep in the forefront of our thinking what it was that brought the adolescent to analysis. Both the analyst and the patient must understand this. Often the adolescent and his environment (his parents, the school, various professional people who have contact with him) will try to get the analyst to forget why the adolescent came for treatment. We have experienced this most often with adolescent patients who have attempted suicide; everyone (including the patient) wants to believe that the event was something that is now past and is best forgotten. We take the view that we cannot forget or pretend, and we let the adolescent know that. By wanting to forget what may have taken place recently, the adolescent is conveying that he knows unconsciously that these events are more painful and more frightening than the long-past ones. But if we allow him to resist understanding his recent past and what it means to his whole life, we encourage him to feel passive toward his past and future, and we deny the patient the possibility of integrating the trauma of the breakdown at puberty and feeling that he can take an active part in creating a continuity to his life.

In analysis, then, reconstruction of the preoedipal or oedipal past makes little sense to the adolescent while he is experiencing failure in his immediate life and while the anxiety is tied to the experiences of puberty and adolescence. His feelings of worthlessness and of being out of control of his present and future sexual life need to make sense to him in the transference before reconstruction of the preadolescent past takes on meaning. Dependence on the analyst, a wish for mothering, a wish to replace the oedipal parent of the same or the opposite sex, early fantasies of having destroyed the parent or a sibling—all may be historically correct, but the interpretations that lead to such reconstructions initially create a feeling in the adolescent that treatment has no meaning. Unless such interpretations and reconstructions are first placed within a context of the adolescent's present sexual life, we lose a central purpose of the treatment which is to undo the experience at puberty that is now distorting the person's age-appropriate experiences and ultimately his sexual body image.

CLINICAL MATERIAL: John

This clinical material is intended to illustrate breakdown and the beginning undoing of the pathology rather than to discuss technique of work. It may seem that the various fantasies of the patient, especially his masturbation fantasies, were easily obtained and readily understood. Of course, this is not so. Caution in obtaining such material cannot be overemphasized; nevertheless, we know that it is possible to put together the content of these fantasies from the patient's associations and behavior as well as from the whole range of derivatives from the unconscious.

John first came for treatment at the age of sixteen. He and his parents felt certain that he was mad or would become mad as he grew older. Psychiatrists had previously considered him to be near-psychotic, but he never had any treatment other than what he described as talks. His parents were quite frantic, making frequent telephone calls pleading with the analyst to treat him.

The family members were not only very worried about John, they had also been terrorized for some years by his behavior— his friendlessness and the accompanying accusation that it was his parents' fault, especially his mother's; his sudden verbal and physical attacks on his mother and his younger sister; his episodes of depression and crying; his refusal to leave the house. By the time he came to treatment the family's feeling was one of last chance.

Although he remembered his latency as a lonely and sad time, John dates the belief that he was mad or was going mad from age thirteen, when a devastating coincidence occurred— the onset of puberty and a decision by the school that he should move to a lower class. At this time he left a note stating that he wanted to kill himself. In fact, he has never attempted suicide, even though there were many occasions during his early adolescence when he felt deadened by his depression and his feelings of worthlessness. During these times he would spend days away from school, refusing to leave the house, sleeping, masturbating, threatening to kill his mother, or just sitting around being cared for by her. The caring took the form of bringing him food, bathing him, and pleading with him to talk about what was worrying him. Although the sadism in his behavior is obvious, the more important factor for understanding his pathology was the extent to which these events or emotions had already been woven into what he and the analyst could establish later as his central masturbation fantasy.

Many of the sessions during the first few months of treatment were taken up with details of John's daily life. The theme of suffering was included in almost every description. His mother was described as a sly manipulator; his father, a man highly regarded in his profession, was mainly idealized and dismissed as being near to perfection; his younger sister was considered to be somewhat stupid and harmless.

John's references to the analyst had to do mainly with the good fortune in being treated by him, with some cautious complaints about the analyst's insistence that John attend five times weekly even though travel took well over an hour each way. John assumed from the start that the analyst considered him mad and that it was for this reason only that the analyst had insisted on John's daily attendance. He reminded the analyst regularly that the analyst was making his suffering worse, but with the added assurance that he did not mind because he was sure it was good for him, a belief that was correct in more ways than one because the suffering person was an important part of the content of his core fantasy. The analyst did not hide his concern for John and his belief that John was a very disturbed young man, but he did tell John early on that he did not consider him mad. The analyst decided to do this because of the quality of John's anxiety revolving around his masturbation and the depression he lived with; in addition, his night fears and his isolation during the first part of the analysis persuaded the analyst to do what Freud intimated was essential with certain kinds of patients—that is, to hold them with one hand while doing surgery with the other. The analyst knew that this way of working might temporarily disturb the development of the transference and might easily play into John's unconscious wish to offer his sexual body to the analyst but felt it necessary to enable John to begin to see the defensive use he was making of behaving in a mad way. Only then would it be possible for John to come nearer to the content of what he felt to be his madness.

The early clues of the impingement on his reality testing of certain fantasy content came initially from John's description of his delight and relief when people recognized and greeted him. It was only much later that he and the analyst could notice that his response to being recognized was much more reassuring to him following masturbation; it then became clear that some of his masturbation fantasies could not be re-repressed too readily and that temporarily following masturbation he could not be sure whether he was the same person he had been before masturbation. He was terrified to talk about this because of his fear that he would lose complete touch with the outside world. The identification with a damaged, humiliated woman was of such intensity during his masturbation that he had to be reassured by people and by the analyst that he had not changed. His weeping in his sessions and his need to run from the subway to the consulting room so as to arrive exhausted were additional clues to some of the content of his core fantasy, but it was through the examination of his need to sit up and see the analyst during his sessions that it was established that John's need to look at people's facial expressions was of central importance to his fantasy life. The paranoid fear was there as well but was not primary. Until his need to look at faces could be established, he simply felt driven to do things without being at all conscious of the presence of any fantasies; and he was certainly not aware of the compelling nature of some of his actions.

This compelling and repetitive quality convinced the analyst that an examination of John's need to look at faces would lead to the content of his core fantasy. Until meaning could be added to the content as well as to the defensive use being made of his present behavior, he would feel out of control and frightened of what he might do to the analyst. His present fantasies, as well as the gratification he was now getting from seeing himself as the isolated and suffering boy, continued to interfere seriously in his ability to use day-to-day experiences as a kind of trial action. His relationships to contemporaries were severely affected—he could not continue any friendships for more than a few weeks; he spent hours alone in his room in the hostel where he lived; he visited sports arenas and spent many hours watching girls straining themselves. When John was able to talk about his masturbation, he began to realize that his need to look at women's or girls' faces had existed *consciously* since the age of seven and that the face in the fantasy had to have a pained expression. This fantasy remained a secret, but only at puberty was the compelling quality added. The breakdown at puberty had manifested itself by sudden brutal attacks on his mother (a number of times to the point that he hurt her seriously) and, at the same time, by the need to avoid girls for fear that he might want to attack or kill them. This breakthrough at puberty of the oedipal wish to attack and sexually assault his mother was very worrying to the analyst diagnostically because it sounded much like an acute psychotic breakthrough, but he felt that the assault also contained the defense against the more direct sexual wish and might therefore be somewhat less ominous.

John also remembered that during this time, soon after puberty, he sometimes believed that he had actually killed his mother—he would have to search the house frantically to find her alive and well. This was reexperienced in the transference following an illness of the analyst—John could not stop talking of what he had done to the analyst and said that there were times during the analyst's absence when he thought he actually had attacked and hurt him; the fact that the analyst maintained telephone contact with John during the illness enabled him to feel convinced that the analyst was well and that John had not harmed him.

The acknowledgment of the fantasy and the analyst's belief, conveyed to John, that the fantasy and the compelling behavior had a meaning that they would in time be able to understand made a critical difference to his day-to-day life; it also gave him hope that something could be done about his illness. Even before the meaning of the fantasy or his actions could be established, his paranoid accusations of people diminished, and he began to be able to concentrate more on his academic work. He also stopped the physical attacks on his mother; this gave him new hope that he might not after all be mad. Although it was not yet possible for the fantasy to be contained within the transference, it was nevertheless possible for the analyst to interpret it in a way that enabled John to feel together they were trying to make sense of something that had damaged his life for years and had created the feeling before treatment that he should be dead or, more correctly, should be killed. The note he had left at age thirteen saying he would kill himself made sense once he could add this meaning of his identification with the victim whose face is contorted in pain. For him, puberty had meant that his sexual wishes were directed also at his father, who was, for John, the person who could attack and gratify him at the same time.

By now, John had acknowledged not only the importance of the fantasy in his compelling behavior but also the extent of his sadness and inner isolation. The concentration in the interpretations of his need to submit to the analyst, to want to give over his body so that the analyst could do with it what he liked (as he felt his mother had done), to want the analyst to attack him, and to want to be the girl whose face is contorted helped make it possible for his crazy behavior to become more and more confined to his sessions. Although he never hit the analyst, he began to shout at him and accuse him of influencing his thoughts. This was John's way of telling the analyst that he was now part of his masturbation fantasy. By shouting he felt he could keep the analyst from getting close to him. His sexual longing for the analyst, instead of having to be denied and creating more anxiety, could begin to make some sense to him. Prognostically, John's ability to confine his crazy behavior to his sessions rather than permit it to encompass his life encouraged the analyst who became more certain that John's psychoticlike functioning was not a sign that his reality testing had been damaged in an irreversible way. It also enabled the analyst to speculate with greater certainty that the damage developmentally to John's mental structure was probably oedipal and there-

fore more readily reversible rather than having existed from
infancy or early childhood, with the resultant distortion in development and structuralization and with the lesser likelihood
of reversibility through treatment.

John described how he needed to masturbate before coming
to his sessions. It was clear from the shame he felt that he
imagined the analyst as the one masturbating him, but it was
still some time before John and the analyst could establish that
this also contained his wish to give the analyst his sexual feelings and his excitement or, more correctly, to make the analyst
responsible for them. The ability to contain or confine much of
his pathology within the transference also had the effect of his
feeling somewhat freer to have close friendships at college. He
began to demand that the analyst take his mad thoughts away
so that he could be like others, which, for him, meant that he
could feel calm when being with a girl.

This material could be understood in a variety of ways, and
here the specific model of mental functioning the analyst uses
will add one meaning or another to the clinical material and to
the interpretations. Although the analyst understood this material within the transference initially as representing the wish
for a homosexual contact with him, feeling forced to submit to
the analyst, and wishing to identify in thought with women or
girls with pained facial expressions, these interpretations were
intended only as preparation for what is much more central to
the understanding and undoing of psychopathology in the adolescent patient. To have stopped with the interpretation and
reconstruction of either the fear or the wish for homosexual
contact would have missed the essential ingredient of adolescent pathology, of which John's pathology was certainly representative. Adding and making more central to the analysis at
this point the understanding through interpretation of John's
wish to offer the analyst his sexual body and make him responsible for that part of his body and mind which he felt was the
producer and carrier of his mad sexual thoughts and feelings,
thereby making the analyst responsible for his self-hatred and
body-hatred, changed the focus of the treatment. It enabled
John and the analyst instead to concentrate on this hatred and

on the responsibility for it, which John tried to hand over to the analyst. This brought back memories of the intrusions into his mind from his mother, which he felt he could not control, partly because of the gratification he got. He recalled how he had himself insisted on being washed or bathed until he was fourteen and how, following the bathing, he would masturbate with the thought of being penetrated sexually by his mother's penis, usually through the anus.

John had by this time been in analysis for three years. He now had a girlfriend and was able to risk having intercourse with her. He described how he had to look into her vagina before being able to penetrate her because of his fear that he might have contact with another penis or that her pained facial expression would make him lose control, and he would then hit her or kill her. He became so frightened that he had to stop seeing her for nearly a month, until he could be sure through treatment that he would not go mad. He asked the analyst to meet his girlfriend, this being his way of offering her to him and of giving up his own sexual body. This led to further memories of watching his mother fall down some stairs when he was about age three, seeing her pained expression and feeling convinced for some years following the experience that this was how she looked when his father "attacked her." During this period of the analysis, his dreams consisted mainly of monsters coming out of holes, people falling out of aircraft and being killed, or people dying. Once when he had dreamed of the analyst hitting him and his pleading for the analyst to stop, he said that his girlfriend had told him she was getting fed up with him. The dream also contained the feeling that his sexuality was now the analyst's and that he was having intercourse with his girlfriend only because the analyst was insisting on it and expecting it of him. This remained a danger, inasmuch as the intercourse was experienced also as a submission to the analyst.

But what began to make sense was that his behavior both in the treatment and outside also carried the wish to attack the analyst and destroy his potency. John's envy and idealization of the analyst represented the defense against the wish to destroy

him as a man and as the person who might give John the potency that for most of his life he did not have and partly did
not want. Developmentally, the idealization of the analyst
pointed to an area of danger because it carried John's passive
submission, with only a slight hint of the presence of an active
process of taking the analyst in.

7
Object Relationships, the Use of the Body, and Transference

Some adolescents demand to be given the experience of having their bodies loved and wanted by the analyst; being understood is not enough. For the less severely disturbed adolescent, to understand the meaning of what he is seeking by making such demands of the analyst can enable him to control the intensity of the demands and the accompanying aggression. The more seriously disturbed adolescent is often unable to use interpretation or understanding to feel in control of his wishes; instead he must feel that his body is actually being loved. In the transference he may use a range of behaviors to force the analyst to gratify this need. But this is not only a transference phenomenon, it is a characteristic of the adolescent's life, which was present well before treatment began. He feels compelled by his anxiety to use his body as part of an object relationship.

The two patients described in this chapter constantly presented the analyst with their need to involve their bodies in the analytic relationship; however, the specific manner differed greatly. Doris, by her impulsive behavior, would get people to care for her and would use her body to announce her distress. Mary responded to all attempts to come close to her either physically or emotionally as intrusive attacks and behaved as if she wished to remain totally isolated from any physical contact and from the analyst.

Descriptively, the first patient, Doris, shared many of the characteristics of those adult patients who come under the classification of "borderline functioning" while the second,

Mary, was nearer to that of "narcissistic personality disorder." But these classifications are not used here in a dynamic or diagnostic sense because they do not take into account the developmental implications of the psychopathologies in adolescence.

CLINICAL MATERIAL

Doris

Doris, aged eighteen, the "borderline" patient, was a potentially attractive young woman, intelligent and artistically creative. When the analyst first saw her, she was tastefully but not strikingly dressed and gave no particular outward indications of being emotionally disturbed. She appeared to relate appropriately to the analyst, although she seemed unable to say why she felt she needed treatment. She was living alone in a room in London. Her parents had separated two years earlier, and her mother had recently begun living with another man. Doris had been referred for psychological treatment by a gynecologist whom she had consulted because of irregular menstruation. Later the analyst learned that her mother had also become worried because, when Doris stayed with her, she refused to eat any meals but then would secretly stuff herself with anything that was available in the house.

In the initial interview the analyst also felt concerned about the vague manner in which she talked about her immediate plans. Despite having no clear idea of what she felt was wrong, she agreed rapidly with the suggestion that she get a part-time job so that she would be able to come at the times the analyst could see her. This showed how eagerly and hungrily she responded to the offer of treatment—as if she felt it was an offer from the analyst to fill her empty life. During the first few months of treatment it became clear that her feeling of emptiness was closely linked to the loss of the old relationship to her mother—because her mother no longer needed her, she was left feeling lost herself.

Doris was the youngest child in a large family and felt that she had always had a very special and close relationship to her mother, different from that of the other siblings. She saw this as reflecting her mother's need because of the unsatisfactory relationship that existed between her parents. More specifically she was aware that this unsatisfactoriness was related to the parents' sexual lives. Although Doris consciously was pleased that her mother was now happy, she also felt terribly jealous of the new man in her mother's life; she no longer was needed by her mother. As she acknowledged these feelings, she talked of what had been her greatest fear when she first left home at sixteen: sitting alone in her room and feeling totally unable to move or do anything. She had told the analyst that she now masturbated when alone, which reassured her that she needed her body for her own needs and not only as something with which to satisfy her mother. She used masturbation to create the fantasy of not being alone or helpless.

As the analysis progressed, Doris began to show her attachment to the analyst more openly, but this was expressed only in her behavior, not in her words. She found it increasingly difficult to leave after her sessions. She implied that she felt helpless and unable to control herself and get home; on a few occasions the analyst had to call a taxi for her. At that time this still seemed part of the ongoing analytic material that was being acted out in the transference. Looking back, however, this can be understood as part of another process that was going on simultaneously and independently of the analytic work. At times the analyst reacted to this by feeling worried and at other times by being uneasy, since it seemed as if the analyst was being repeatedly put on the spot in her effort to maintain an analytic distance from the patient. For instance, Doris would come into the room, go casually over to the bookcase and pick up a book and comment on it, wanting the analyst to reply. She would ask to borrow a book or just walk around the room looking at other things and picking them up. She might suddenly sit up and face the analyst during the session, or, after a long silence, she would get up and walk out. This was all done with an air of casual innocence that appeared to deny completely the implication of her actions, dismissing any attempts at understanding her behavior. At the time, the analyst felt that this behavior contained all of Doris's aggression against her. Now it can be understood as Doris's actual inability to keep to the analytic framework during those times when she felt unable to contain her anxiety.

Yet, throughout this period, she brought in material in the form of dreams and associations, and the analytic work appeared to be proceeding. Her behavior seemed motivated by the need to involve the analyst more directly with herself and with her actual body. Later, when she became more manifestly disturbed, her behavior became increasingly unpredictable. Once, instead of leaving the analyst's home after a session (where the consulting took place), she wandered off, found a piano in another room, and started playing it. Another time the analyst came home late at night and found Doris lying in the road, apparently in a semidrugged state, and the analyst had to take her to a hospital. Looking back again, these events can be understood as a gradual intrusion of Doris's body into the analytic relationship, as a constant demand that the analyst should accept Doris's wish for care and stimulation of her body, and as experiencing the analyst's efforts to keep an analytic distance via interpretations as a rejection of her body and implied disapproval of her wishes.

Her day-to-day relationships were characterized by the same apparent vagueness and denial of any conscious motivation. She talked of the ideal relationship she had had with a man the year before she started treatment. This was probably her first important relationship with a man. Although she mentioned that this man had now left London and the relationship had ended, she was clearly denying the extent of her distress. The only way she could communicate it to the analyst was by cutting off her hair, which had played an important role in the relationship as something the man admired in her. She described the relationship as ideal because they never made any fixed arrangements to meet; whenever she wanted to be with him, they would just happen to bump into each other in the street.

During her analysis she lived alone in a part of London where many other lonely young people drifted around. She said she had many friends, but she described these relation-ships in such a vague and idealized way that the analyst had no real picture of the ever-changing people. Doris seemed to par-ticipate in whatever sexual or drug-taking activity suggested to her; she was unable to feel critical of or discriminatory about the activity or the person involved. The wish to have her body accepted and not to be alone with it seemed to overcome any other feelings she might have.

When the analysis began to get closer to her feelings and anxieties about sexual relationships, Doris acted out dramati-cally. She spoke of having been unable to allow herself to be penetrated by the man she had been fond of, but said that they had practiced fellatio together. The day after she had been able to talk of this, the analyst was contacted by a psychiatric unit where Doris had been taken because her employer had be-come frightened by her odd behavior. All Doris could tell the hospital staff was the analyst's telephone number. She stayed in the hospital for a short period, keeping contact with the analyst by phone. She was diagnosed at that time as schizophrenic. When the analyst saw her again, Doris told her that she had swallowed a great deal of hash that day and had been unable to function or communicate, but she had still known exactly what was happening to her. On the phone she could only repeatedly say yes. This worrying episode raised the question of the de-gree to which Doris was functioning on a psychotic level, even though her behavior might be understood as the acting out of her sexual experience and of how out of control it made her feel.

She then began to have intercourse, which included being penetrated, but this did not stop her from taking part in per-verse sexual activities. The need for this behavior was specifi-cally related to the compulsive repetition of earlier childhood experiences. As a child she had been close to her slightly older brother, with whom she had been continuously involved in mu-tual masturbatory games and activities. She blamed her mother for never having made any attempt to stop them, even though it had all been done quite openly. The only thing her mother could not tolerate, she said, was any anger directed at her.

Doris's father also appeared to have acted in a very seductive manner. He walked around naked in front of the children; when Doris awoke early in the morning, he would encourage her to come into his bed and hold her close to his body, telling her that she must not wake her mother.

Doris now repeated these experiences with a girl and her boyfriend, both of whom she had met at the hospital. She masturbated the girl in front of the boyfriend and watched the girl and her boyfriend having intercourse. She identified with the girl's sexual demands on her and derived pleasure from feeling needed in the same passive uncritical way that she had previously felt with her male acquaintances. The analyst's role was constantly to try to mobilize Doris's awareness of her own feelings, and thus of her own body, and to help her not to respond as if she were completely helpless and without wishes or needs of her own. She was now acting out her wish to offer herself to the analyst in whatever way the analyst would want.

It is not possible to know whether analysis would have succeeded in allowing Doris to feel more in touch with her own body and feelings had analysis continued without interruption. But two years after her analysis started, Doris's mother suddenly died. At this point, Doris and the analyst had been able to reconstruct her intense longing for physical closeness to her mother and to relate her present hatred of her mother and of herself to feeling excluded in favor of a man, implying that her body could not offer equal satisfaction. After the mother's death the analyst's main effort was to help Doris to mourn her. At the time it seemed as if analysis did help her work through some of the depression and anger with her mother for leaving her completely; she even began to experience some relief about feeling freer from her tie to her mother.

Again, another process was going on simultaneously. This could first be seen in Doris's wish to hold the analyst's hand in the session. Unconsciously her wish was that the analyst should need to hold Doris's hand. She told the analyst how, when she was little, she used to sit under the table and secretly fondle her mother's hand while her mother went on talking to other grown-ups. Her fantasy was that her mother really needed her rather than the people she was talking to. Doris was now haunted by the thought that her mother's body had been cremated, her hand was no longer available, and her mother did not need her. In all her dreams she now was in the sea, with or without her mother, floating and being engulfed; the dreams contained all her longing for her mother and the wish for physical union and closeness with her. In the transference, she demanded that the analyst replace the loss of her mother in reality. She became increasingly uncontrolled and had aggressive outbursts when she felt forced by the analyst to leave at the end of the session. A crisis was reached in a session when she sat up and began to rock in a masturbatory way, then banged her head against the wall so violently that the analyst had to intervene for fear that she would hurt herself. (Her mother had died of a cerebral clot.) She talked of wanting to masturbate, and when the analyst suggested that she try not to but instead talk of her feelings about it, she became violent and was so out of control that the analyst had to hold her and have her taken to a hospital.

This crisis, which temporarily brought analysis to an end, appeared to result from her inability to use masturbation to experience in fantasy the union with her mother's body, with a resulting loss of control of her violence against the analyst who represented the depriving mother who no longer needed Doris. It was clear at the time that the real danger lay in her directing the violence against her own body because she experienced it as useless. She had not been able to prevent her mother from dying, and now only death could reunite her with her mother's body.

While Doris was in the hospital, she again remained in daily contact with the analyst by phone. At the same time the analyst continued to visit weekly to help Doris maintain a sense of reality about what was happening to her. The analyst was aware that the telephone calls enabled Doris to feel that through "creating" the analyst's voice for herself by dialing the telephone number, she was also able to maintain the fantasy of having made the analyst into her real mother and denying any sense of loss as the result of her actions. The analyst was concerned, therefore, about how Doris would react to the next holiday break when the analyst would not be available. Despite the analyst's awareness and the hospital's cooperation, interpretations were not enough to deal with the violence and despair that were precipitated by the announcement of the forthcoming holiday. Doris made a serious suicide attempt, but, discovered in time, her life was saved.

Mary

Mary,[1] like Doris, made a suicide attempt and had an eating disturbance. She was referred for analysis while she was an in-patient in a psychiatric unit following the suicide attempt. She was aged eighteen at the time. While she was in the unit, she had remained completely withdrawn and isolated from the other patients and staff. She was a slightly built, timid girl who looked much younger than her age and spoke so quietly that she could barely be heard. When the analyst first saw her, she kept herself completely hidden in her coat, which she seldom removed. When she talked of what had made her want to die, she mentioned feeling that her body was disgusting and that she was terribly ashamed of it. Before her suicide attempt she had been unable to control a compulsive need to stuff herself secretly with food at night, and this had made her feel fat and repulsive. Later the analyst learned that during the initial period in the hospital after her suicide attempt, Mary had refused to eat and had become so thin that there had been concern about her being anorexic. She herself told the analyst that she felt compelled to make herself thin in order to be able to go on living. Thus, unconsciously she had used her ability to refuse food as a way of reassuring herself that she could maintain control of her body and its demands to be able to feel she could like it. Any outward indication that she no longer was in control of her body made her feel unacceptable and disgusting, bringing with it the threat of her violence being directed against herself or against the object that she saw as responsible for the loss of control. In the transference the analyst was iden-

---

1. This patient's treatment is described in chapter 8.

tified with an intrusive object who could make her lose control, while she desperately sought to remain in control of her feelings and thoughts.

The analyst's only value to her at that time was that she represented a defense against Mary's regressive wish to have her body controlled by her mother, the intruder against whom her violence was directed. She enlisted the analyst's help in not having to return to her home after she left the hospital, but she insisted that the analyst not tell her mother that it was her own wish. She used the fantasy that she had been able to make her mother feel useless by showing that she now had the analyst to care for her. Mary talked of having felt as a child that her mother did not take sufficient care of her body—she had not washed Mary's hair often enough or put cream on her skin. She remembered that when she was fifteen she had felt that she could now care for her own body and that she could do this better than her mother had. At that time she also decided to leave home to become independent of her mother but had felt despairingly that she would starve if she did so.

In her behavior toward the analyst, Mary alternated between creating omnipotent fantasies to make her feel big and powerful when she no longer needed the analyst and being consumed with rage when these fantasies were challenged by her reality. At the same time she felt totally helpless and dependent on an all-powerful but intrusive mother to whom she needed to give in so as to fulfill her own needs. She defended against awareness of her needs by making her body feel "dead." She expressed her dependence on her mother only through her need for approval; it was as if she could control her body but not her fear of rejection.

After she had gone out once with a boy, Mary refused to see him again because she felt that her mother had not approved of her choice. But she also felt afraid of her wish to be kissed. She had always been an exceptionally good and obedient child and had fulfilled her mother's high academic expectations of her. She could not quite understand how her older brother managed so well without the mother's help. Her mother had devoted her life to making Mary into the perfect child. At first

Mary was able to come to her sessions only if accompanied by her mother. Although now aged eighteen, she was dressed in clothes that made her look like a little girl.

In the hospital setting she tried to identify with the other young patients in order to feel more normal. Being a patient in a hospital meant no longer being mother's perfect child—a thought that gave her hope. Feeling that she must have a boyfriend, she attached herself quite unrealistically to a male patient and made plans to go and live with him. She tried to copy other patients so as to feel like them. She threw and broke things when they did, went to a grocery store with them to steal, and finally allowed one of the female patients into her bed. But the analyst did not understand the meaning of this behavior until much later.

Her involvement with other people appeared real only when it contained the demand to be protected against experiences that, in fantasy, were felt to be intrusive attacks on her body. When she went home for a visit and was alone with her mother, she became overwhelmed by the fear that her mother was trying to poison her. She saw her mother as jealous of her and of her relationship to her father. But the only relationship to men, including her father, that Mary could allow consisted of long intense "talks," which were meant to make both her mother and the analyst feel jealous and excluded. Her body played no part in any relationship to men.

Mary appeared to be engaged in a constant battle, both with her mother and with the analyst in the transference, to take over control of her own body rather than have to feel dependent on the object. After a year of analysis Mary said she had had a totally new experience. She could now feel what it was like to be hungry and then choose to eat, rather than eat because it was time to do so. Making her body feel dead and without needs appeared to be her only defense against experiencing her wish to be intruded on by her mother or the analyst. As for her suicide attempt, she said that there had been no particular reason for its timing; she had already felt dead for the previous two years, so it made no difference to kill herself.

For Mary, suicide was the only way she could express her

wish to feel that her body belonged to her—to do with it what she wanted. Suicide represented the only way of removing herself from her mother and at the same time controlling the wish to give in to her. (Doris, on the other hand, saw suicide as the only means of reuniting her body with that of her mother and remaining a part of her.)

Later Mary told the analyst that she could talk only if she had previously decided that the problem was something the analyst could help her with; otherwise there was no point in speaking of it. This attitude represented her wish to control the analyst so that she could continue to experience the analyst as protecting her. Only in this way could she feel safe and in control of her violence against the analyst. When she became more conscious of how compelled she felt to keep certain thoughts secret from the analyst, she wrote a letter to explain what her thoughts were. In the letter she described fantasies of being given an enema by a man or by herself. She said the fantasies were due to her obsession with a memory of her mother giving her an enema when she was four years old. She added that, having told the analyst this, it must now be clear why she hated her body so much and urged that the analyst burn the letter. She responded with cold silence to all attempts to discuss the letter in the sessions. Eventually she exclaimed in an angry voice that the analyst should by now realize that she had no wish to talk about this matter and could not do so.

This feeling was so intense and real for her that months later, when she described a dream in which there was a pile of manure, she remarked that it had been a tremendous effort to bring herself even to say such a word as "manure" to the analyst. The analyst saw this as Mary's fear of losing control over her physical excitement in the session; by not talking of potentially exciting thoughts, she could continue to keep her body dead and separate from the analyst. Her conscious fantasy of a man or herself giving her the enema contained the defense against her wish to give her body to her mother or a woman.

She actually controlled her body as completely as she did her thoughts and feelings. Most of the time she was quite rigid, still, and silent. When she was very tense, she might begin the session by being restless and clearly showing that she was under some physical tension to speak, but she would soon restrain herself and become totally still again, as if dead. It was quite uncanny at times to hear her running eagerly up the steps of the analyst's house, arriving early for her session as if she could not wait to tell the analyst something, and after a few restless movements remain silent for the whole session. Her need to be in control was expressed not only in her silence and body rigidity within the session but also at times by staying away.

When she first left the hospital, she became involved with a boy in the hostel where she was living. She stayed up late at night talking to him, but she could tell the analyst only the number of hours she had spent with him, not what had been said or done. She became manifestly more and more disturbed and unable to function at her work or at the hostel, while she continued to maintain a stubborn secrecy about what was going on. It was clear that the more she clung to her secret the more frightened she became of the analyst. Because of her continued defiance and her fantasy of the analyst as the raping woman, Mary eventually became so frightened of the analyst that she was unable to come to the sessions, having to stay at the hostel all day clinging to the warden. She could not be left alone at night. The analyst had to arrange for her to go back to the hospital, where she stayed for some months.

During the next period of analysis, as Mary gained some sense of independence from the analyst, she acted out her fantasy that she could now dominate and control the analyst completely. She stayed away from sessions without informing the analyst before or after why she had done so. No interpretation could interfere with the obvious gratification she obtained from feeling that she could make the analyst be available whenever she wanted rather than having to feel as if the analyst was in control of her. She ignored all references the analyst made to her behavior and acted as if she were totally unaware that the analyst had any feelings. Previously in the analysis she used to say hopelessly, "But you must have feelings about what I tell you. That's why I can't risk telling you things." Now she acted out her wish that the analyst's feelings did not affect her behavior in any way—what she wanted to show the analyst and her-self was that she no longer needed the analyst's approval. Clearly, she had now reversed the old situation with her mother. Now she could experience the satisfaction she felt her mother had obtained from being in control of her.

Mary's demands on the analyst, although less obvious than Doris's, were no less intense. The analyst was paid to have no feelings or opinions of her own, and she had to sit and be bored if Mary had nothing to say or if Mary did not come. When she did come, her silence in the sessions also took on a new quality. She would come but then would fall asleep for most of the hour. The analyst had to remain still and silent. If the analyst tried to talk about it, Mary dismissed all interpreta-tions and said she was just tired. At the time it seemed that this behavior was her way of defensively controlling the analyst, but gradually it became clearer that she was beginning to enjoy the feeling of complete union with the analyst while she lay asleep in a fetal position. The analyst was there for her if she wanted to talk to her; and all the feelings aroused by outside stimuli, either in Mary's life or in the analyst's, which she experienced as threatening her wish for complete union with the analyst, were now under her control via sleep. Neither she nor the ana-lyst was to have any feelings through talking, but she could now feel safe in being joined to the analyst via both their "dead" bodies.

She responded to holiday breaks very differently from Doris—not with uncontrolled violence and anger and a wish for physical closeness but with depression and by becoming ill. When the analyst interpreted Mary's illness as her wish for the analyst to take physical care of her, she said that she hated be-ing fussed over when she was ill and just wanted to be left alone. She did, in fact, regard illness as a failure to control her body and as something that made her body potentially unac-ceptable and disgusting to the object. As a child she had had repeated nightmares of having her body covered with boils and, in associating to this, referred to herself as an "untouch-able leper."

Her relationships outside the analysis at first were very unreal. She would let herself have intense feelings for a boy she saw on the train and whom she could keep as a fantasy-object, while the boys she went out with had no emotional significance to her. In real relationships she was terrified of being touched, which she experienced as an intrusion into her body that could make her lose control over her aggression. She was afraid that she would attack and kick a boy who entered her room without warning her. She was afraid that if someone in a crowd pushed against her she might lose control and kick that person. She had dreams of breaking off men's genitals. Yet she accepted these feelings without any real anxiety, explaining that she had been told that even as a baby she could not bear to be touched by strangers; this seemed to have reinforced the fantasy she shared with her mother of their exclusive relationship.

Mary felt depressed and anxious when she was without a boyfriend. She said it was not because she minded being alone but because she minded going out alone and being seen alone. But then she felt anxious at the thought that people might look at the boy rather than at her. Thus, she could obtain gratification of her body only from being looked at rather than from being touched. She expressed the same feeling when she talked of never wanting babies because they were too demanding and never gave anything in return. But then she added, "Except if it is a pretty baby."

Her need to keep her relationships with boys nonsexual was consciously related to her fear of losing her virginity. She felt that being a virgin was the only good thing she would have to offer a man; she had to keep her virginity in order to find a man who would "deserve" to have her. However, she continued to feel that she must try to have relationships with men for fear of being regarded as abnormal. She invited a man she met casually into her room at night; and when he tried to approach her, she fought him off. She came to the session in a manic state, triumphant that she had now proved she could withstand a man's attempt to rape her.

As Mary began to feel her body was alive, she was compelled, like Doris, to use it in her relationship to the object, but she used it to reassure herself that she still was in total control of her own and the other person's bodies. In the transference she could allow herself to feel that she needed the analyst only after a long period of defiant staying away and then telephoning to say that she had decided to end her analysis. She said that she had had to experience the feeling of actually having lost the analysis before she could have any feelings about how much she needed it. Apparently, she felt safe to experience feelings only when she was alone and therefore not risking rejection. Doris, on the other hand, was panic-stricken when she was left alone with her body and her feelings about it. When she once developed a stomachache she could not allow the analyst to leave her and held her when the analyst tried to go. Doris, unlike Mary, experienced her body as a means of feeling united with the object; whereas Mary could see her body only as a potential threat to being rejected and could risk bringing it into a relationship only if it were "dead" and thus totally controlled (Bak 1939; Freud 1917).

On a libidinal level, both Doris and Mary had regressed to an oral mode of expressing their libidinal wishes, but there was a very important difference. Doris, with all her uncontrolled, impulsive behavior, seemed to express not only an oral demandingness and greed but also the wish to repeat an earlier form of intense satisfaction. Even her first sexual experience was an unconscious attempt to regain the mother's breast and deny the existence of the penis. Similarly, her anger was always related to feeling frustrated by a lack of gratification in her immediate life, inducing her to find means of recreating the earlier satisfaction for herself on an autoerotic level—that is, without the dependence on the object (Freud 1914; Kernberg 1980; Klein 1958). Thus, although her suicide attempt contained the attack on the analyst for leaving her, it was also an attempt to deny the reality and to feel that she could achieve the intensely satisfying relationship she wanted with the analyst through her own activity.

In contrast, Mary consistently starved herself of all pleasurable experiences in her life, as if to avoid reexperiencing an earlier painful sense of frustration. Her compulsive eating before her suicide attempt expressed her hatred of herself for losing control of her needs and at the same time confirmed her hopelessness about ever finding satisfaction in the future. Unconsciously her expectation could only be for more painful frustration and disappointment. She constantly felt threatened by her overwhelming aggression and hatred, which she could control only by silence and immobility. The aggression also represented the wish to starve and frustrate the analyst in retaliation for her own frustration. It was as if she felt that the only satisfaction she could achieve was by turning her passive experience into an active one. As a result of the analyst's attempt to show her how she was starving herself of the relief that analytic work could give her, Mary could allow herself to begin to have some hope in the future (Blos 1972; Ferenczi 1911). This suggests that in her infancy she had actually experienced more painful frustrations of her bodily needs than satisfying experiences; then, as an adolescent, she was unable to endure the hatred she felt when she saw what others had achieved, and what she had no hope of achieving with her sexual body. She could only repeat the fantasy of her mother's getting all the satisfaction while she had none; her suicide was the only way of depriving her mother.

While the overt behavior of these two patients showed many similarities, the differences in the underlying meaning point to differences in their development. From these we would conclude that the adolescent who functions on a borderline level reacts to the sense of loss engendered by the change of body image with a compulsive attempt to repeat an earlier, intensely satisfying physical relationship to the original object. This brings with it a constant vulnerability to loss of control over the aggression against the new object when the actual experience does not fulfill the fantasy experience (Jacobson 1971; Ritvo 1981).

In comparison, the adolescent who functions on the level of narcissistic personality disorder shows a mode of functioning related to the need to defend against frustration and disappointment of libidinal needs and the inability to change as the result of puberty. The aggression that such adolescents fear they cannot control represents the wish to retaliate for the lack of gratification and the pain of the feeling of emptiness. Having no hope of obtaining libidinal satisfaction from a new object after the pubertal changes, they need to create a feeling of narcissistic self-sufficiency. The only source of narcissistic cathexis is through complete submission to the demands of the superego (Erlich 1978; Rosenfeld 1964; Katan 1954).

We may also use these assumptions to speculate about the genesis of another characteristic feature of borderline pathology—that is, the patient's inability to maintain any sublimatory activity. In line with the view just presented, this could be seen as a rejection of any activity that does not have the unconsciously searched-for intensity of pleasurable bodily experience. In structural terms, for the borderline patient we see the result of a particularly intense libidinal investment of the body image and a corresponding sense of loss at puberty. In the patient with a narcissistic personality disorder, by contrast, we see the result of a lack of an earlier satisfactory libidinal investment of the body image, with a subsequent defensive attempt to compensate by the premature use of the superego as a substitute source of satisfaction, a dependence on sublimations for achieving satisfaction, and an intense wish to take over the role of the depriving object as a way of trying to undo the earlier frustrations that were unconsciously linked with passivity.

8
Attempted Suicide in Adolescence:
A Psychotic Episode

Attempted suicide—the result of a conscious decision to kill oneself—rarely occurs before puberty but becomes a real possibility in the seriously disturbed person from puberty on. Many adolescents who talk of having thoughts of killing themselves say that they first had such thoughts at fourteen or fifteen years of age but rarely during childhood. A special meaning must attach itself to attempted suicide that is specifically determined by the onset of puberty. An action that is carried out with the conscious thought that it will result in one's own death must be viewed very differently from other forms of self-inflicted injury. Many of the manifest pathologies of vulnerable adolescents carry some risk to their lives—anorexia, wrist slashing, compulsive involvement in dangerous activities, drug taking—but these forms of behavior do not include the conscious wish to die and therefore would not, from a developmental point of view, have the same significance for the adolescent. A suicide attempt, however minor, always represents a temporary loss of the ability to maintain the link to external reality and must be viewed as an acute psychotic episode. However sane the adolescent believes he was at the time of the attempt, there is no objective reality attached to the idea of his own death. Instead the action is totally determined by a fantasy that excludes any awareness of the reality of his death.

At the time of the decision to kill himself, the adolescent's body is no longer part of him but instead becomes the object that can express all his feelings and fantasies. At that moment, conscious guilt has no meaning. The adolescent who injures himself, by constrast, is still able to be in touch with the objective reality of his body through the physical experiences of pain or vision as well as in his wish to share this experience with an outside observer.

The adolescent who intends to kill himself is experiencing a particular relationship to his body. The ability or wish to protect his body from external physical danger or from his own hatred and attack on it has become severely impaired. The body has instead become totally identified with the fantasied attacker who must now be silenced.

ATTEMPTED SUICIDE AND DEVELOPMENTAL BREAKDOWN

Puberty normally invokes the incest barrier between the child and parent. The adolescent must look for ways of finding gratification of his sexual and narcissistic needs apart from the parents. But the adolescent who, for whatever historical reason, is unable to form relationships and loses all hope that he can eventually find a means toward an effective resolution of his anxiety and tension is vulnerable to experiencing the physically mature, sexual body as the source of his anxiety and hatred.

We always view a suicide attempt in adolescence as a sign of an acute breakdown in the process toward the establishment of a stable sexual identity. A state of developmental deadlock has been reached. The developmental process has come to a halt, and the adolescent feels that there is no longer any possibility either for progressive development toward adulthood or for a regressive move to dependence on the oedipal objects. The suicide attempt is often immediately preceded by an event that represents failure in the move away from his dependent relationship to the parents.

In some patients studied, the fear of failure in an important exam or the inability to decide whether to leave home to attend college was part of the external circumstances that precipitated the suicide attempt.[1] In other patients the failure was directly

1. This study, using data from psychoanalytic treatment, was carried out at the Centre for Research into Adolescent Breakdown, London.

linked to the experience of having failed in a heterosexual relationship, with the result that the adolescent felt that he had no
way of freeing himself from his dependence on his parents for
his sexual gratification and unconsciously from the anxiety due
to the incestuous meaning of his wishes. In each case the adolescent felt caught up in an unbearable conflict and totally
helpless to find some *active* means out of the conflict. But the
conflict seemed different for the male and the female patients.
The male adolescent felt that he had to submit passively to the
father for help, but unconsciously this submission was also a
means of controlling his violence; for the female adolescent,
the fear of being forced back to dependence on her mother
aroused intense hostility, with the added fear of losing control
of the violence against her mother.

The need to find some active means of dealing with the
sense of passive submission was expressed by all the adolescents
studied by turning to someone outside the family for help. But
they unconsciously had already given up hope because they believed that nobody could help them feel less of a failure if they
could not be different from what they now were. They saw
themselves as unwanted and useless. Their bodies represented
and contained their abnormal sexual thoughts and wishes. No
amount of help or reassurance from the person they turned to
was sufficient to undo this inner sense of badness and sexual
abnormality. The effort to get help or reassurance had, in each
instance, resulted in confirming the adolescent's belief that nobody could help him, that only some action on his own part
could undo the helplessness he was experiencing. Their attack
on their bodies was experienced as a relief because it enabled
them to feel there was something they could do. Some talked
of having felt a longing to achieve a sense of "peace and noth-
ingness" and so undo the state of painful tension they were in.
Unconsciously their suicidal act also expressed hatred of their
mature sexual body.

SIGNS OF RISK

The treatment of adolescents who have made serious attempts
to kill themselves has enabled us to make use of certain obser-

vations in our assessment work to decide when there is an immediate risk to their lives. The danger of an actual attempt may be most acute when, in addition to an external situation that represents deadlock, there appears to be no conscious guilt attached to the idea of what the adolescent's parents or the analyst would feel at his death. The long-standing fear of abandonment and rejection turns into a conviction that he was not wanted or loved and that his parents or the analyst would be relieved if he were dead. It is as if the adolescent has already destroyed everybody and everything good inside himself.

A serious risk may be present when we observe that the adolescent has given up the struggle. An example is the adolescent who no longer makes any effort at establishing relationships. Instead, he remains exposed to his dependence on his parents and is unable to prevent his body from continuing its development toward adulthood. This can be one of the reasons why significant birthdays, such as eighteen or twenty-one, can become the "external basis" for a suicide attempt. Unconsciously the body becomes hated and attacked because it is seen as something that exposes him to the shame he feels about himself.

Such adolescents may show the first signs of risk when they feel unable to control the impulse to attack one of the parents. Frank, aged nineteen, felt constantly threatened by fantasies of attacking his father. At work he was quite unable to talk to any of the girls for fear of revealing himself as unmasculine and childish. The times when he actually came close to violence against his father were when he longed for his father's company but was then compelled to provoke him into some sign of irritation by dependent clinging. Frank saw his wish to attack his father as a means of showing his father that he could now dominate him and did not have to submit to him. The awareness of how near he came to acknowledging that he could kill his father made Frank feel that he had to kill himself. Only in this way, he felt, would he be able to control his potentially murderous rage. Killing himself could also be understood as killing the body that contained the wishes and fantasies which, if allowed into consciousness, would face Frank with his sexual longing for his father. Such adolescents may talk of their parents dying before them; for them even a minor physical illness in a parent can precipitate a suicide attempt.

The adolescent who appears to have failed or who has given up the effort to move away from the parents as the objects of his libidinal needs and wishes remains vulnerable to suicidal thoughts. But the one who is at risk experiences his body in some acute sense as a prison from which he must escape—as if the body must be controlled and subjugated. For this reason, the adolescent who is aware of feeling aroused by someone of the same sex, or who feels that he must masturbate even though it makes him feel a failure or abnormal, may be at risk. Part of the risk lies in feeling that there is no way out, that he *is* abnormal, or that he is no longer in control of his own life and thoughts. A number of adolescents who had attempted suicide spoke of a sense of calm and relief after they had swallowed the pills; it was only when they began to experience the physical effects of the pills that they became anxious and sought help. The calmness and relief can also be a sign that the long-standing guilt and self-hatred have been removed by the decision to die.

This state of depersonalization at the time of the suicide attempt may also help to explain why so many adolescents readily reassure themselves and us that it was just a silly impulse, which they will not repeat. We learned from their treatment that their awareness of being able to put their suicidal thoughts into action became a secret source of strength for them. The fantasy was of having a secret weapon that now enabled them to go on living because it was always available as a means of avoiding pain. We place great importance, both in assessment and in treatment, on keeping the reality of the potential danger of suicide in the forefront. This is the only safeguard available when assessing or treating. Both the adolescent and the analyst have to be aware that a risk to the life of the adolescent exists; without such recognition there is a constant danger of colluding with the adolescent's secret omnipotent fantasy of the suicidal act. Equally important, of course, the adolescent must know that even if the analyst is aware of the danger, the analyst cannot stop him from killing himself.

TREATMENT ISSUES

During the treatment of the adolescent who has attempted suicide, certain danger signs can be used to predict the risk of another suicide attempt or the possibility of premature ending of the treatment. We learned of the vulnerability of such adolescents to experiencing any separation from the analyst, including weekend or holiday breaks, as an abandonment that confirmed their belief in their worthlessness and increased their hatred of themselves. So long as the adolescent was being seen regularly by the analyst, it seemed as if feelings of self-hatred or despair or the giving in to a sense of hopelessness about the potential for change could be experienced more safely, and the meaning and historical source of these feelings in the adolescent's life could be located. As soon as a holiday break approached, thoughts of death or suicide tended to return. Understanding the anger provoked by the experience of being left can help the adolescent survive the holiday and weekend breaks in treatment without needing to express the anger by an attack on his body. We also found that some adolescents instead developed psychosomatic illnesses over the holiday break. Others became involved in transient sexual relationships that lost meaning as soon as the analyst returned. This observation confirmed our original assumption that some impairment exists in the ability of these adolescents to relate to their bodies in a caring manner. Being left was experienced as a physical abandonment that, if it could not be undone by finding a sexual partner, led to the psychosomatic expression of the depressive feelings.

The adolescents we have observed in analytic treatment were all concerned about, and in some cases convinced they were, developing in some sexually abnormal way. They felt that their bodies were responsible for their conviction that the future held no expectation for them of pleasurable achievement, either in a physically sexual sense or in terms of their self-esteem or narcissism. They felt unable to achieve normal relationships and often were unable to see themselves as parents in the future. They could not experience any hope. Unconsciously, they not only had given up hope but were tormented by hatred of whatever they did perceive in themselves—a feeling that was strengthened through their awareness of those sexual or aggressive feelings or thoughts that they themselves judged as evidence of abnormality or unlovableness. They thought they deserved to be punished.

By locating these feelings in their bodies, they could then experience death both as a fantasy of punishing themselves and as the end of their suffering and, thus, the fulfillment of a wish. It was as if their bodies represented the predicament they felt themselves to be in. By having become sexually potent, the body was responsible for their inability to return to the relative safety of their more passive childhood ways of relating to their parents, teachers, and now, their therapists. At the same time they were unsure that they could find in new adult relationships a reliable way of achieving satisfaction. Anything that evoked dependence on the analyst, such as awareness of the relief from anxiety that treatment could offer them, was experienced as something shameful that had to be denied to themselves and others because it was felt as containing their regressive, passive wishes to be physically held and stimulated. In their relationship to the analyst they not only constantly expected to be left and rejected but also unconsciously needed to provoke rejection through their actions as a way of expressing their own rejection of themselves. This was repeatedly reenacted in the relationship to the analyst and contained a repetition of the dynamic meaning of the actual suicide attempt.

Most of the adolescents, as we have mentioned, had turned to someone for help prior to the attempt, but the help they had been offered became totally distorted through their own perception of themselves. The "helper" had become the persecutor who was held responsible for the adolescent's own intense feelings of shame and failure and who was then "attacked" in the fantasy through the suicidal act. For instance, some adolescents who had been offered therapeutic help in response to their suicide attempts tried to kill themselves a second time because they could see the offer of therapeutic help only as a confirmation of their abnormality and as something shameful (Deutsch 1968; Katan 1950; Schilder 1935).

The adolescents' inability to experience any painful feelings and their need to locate them as coming from outside themselves seriously impair their ability to form any sort of lasting relationships. Their only defense against their expectation of being rejected or left is by turning it into an action that inflicts the painful feelings on the other person. Often they cannot wait to be left by the analyst at a holiday break but instead will stay away just before the holiday or arrange to have a vacation before the analyst's return. These are often the patients who tend to be silent for long periods, making the analyst into the one who has to experience being alone and without support instead of having to risk feeling this way themselves. Unconsciously they then experience the analyst's silence as proof that the analyst no longer cares about them or even wishes that they were dead.

These adolescents cannot allow themselves to enjoy themselves in a temporarily regressive way—instead they are constantly haunted by the search for achievements that allow them to feel free of self-reproach. Their relationships are equally colored by the search for someone to make their sexual body perfect and beyond criticism, which they unconsciously believe to be impossible. Thus it tends to be the apparently successful and academically ambitious adolescent or the promiscuous girl who is vulnerable to making a suicide attempt. But the others who are vulnerable are those adolescents who show signs of already having given up the struggle, who no longer make any effort at establishing relationships, and who are left exposed to giving in to the wish to remain totally dependent on their parents for reassurance.

ADDITIONAL COMMENTS ON TREATMENT

A suicide attempt in adolescence represents a serious interference in the development to adulthood and is a sign of urgent need for psychological help. This is so whether the suicide attempt was recent or occurred in the past. Even when daily treatment is not available, a more limited form of therapy can often be effective. By helping the adolescent understand what it is that made him feel compelled to attack his own body, we can help him to feel once again in control of his life and his future. Since we view the actual suicide attempt as an acute psychotic episode in the life of the adolescent, we see it as constituting a traumatic experience in which the anxiety he was experiencing had become completely overwhelming. The effect of this trauma creates the need for the adolescent to repeat and reenact situations that dynamically are equivalent to a suicidal act. By enabling the adolescent to reexperience and relive the trauma in the transference, the destructive power of the traumatic experience can be lessened.

We can define some therapeutic criteria that are essential for effective change to take place. One such criterion is the need for the stability of the setting in which the help is being offered. The help must be thought of as long-term, and must be consistent and totally reliable in resisting all efforts on the part of the adolescent to disrupt it or to look for alternative ways of feeling better. The analyst must be constantly alert to any decisions about changes in the adolescent's life that are presented as positive moves but that can then be used by the adolescent as an alternative to treatment and as a resistance to change. The reality of the suicidal act, the danger to life, and the possibility of its repetition because of its internally determined compelling quality must be kept constantly in the forefront of the adolescent's and the analyst's thoughts until the meaning and the experience of the suicide attempt have been worked through (Freud 1910, 1914; Stewart 1963). The analyst will be under constant pressure both from the adolescent and from himself to help the adolescent to forget or deny the experience.

The adolescent, at the beginning of treatment, is totally dependent on the analyst to allow and enable him to become conscious of the guilt, shame, and self-hatred and, in this way, to help him undo the traumatic effect of the experience of the suicide attempt, however minor the attempt may seem to have been. Although it is terrifying for the adolescent to have to recognize that he was temporarily mad and was acting from an inner compulsion, we see treatment as the only means by which the traumatic effect of such a psychotic episode can be worked through. Once an adolescent has attempted suicide, he unconsciously believes that he has killed a part of himself; he creates and perpetuates the fantasy that *this dead part now exists inside his body*. This dead part must be located and defined during treatment, and the meaning of its presence must be understood.

When we have recommended treatment for adolescents who made a serious suicide attempt, we have often been surprised at the difficulty in convincing the adolescent, his parents, and the professional worker involved (teacher, doctor, social worker) of the need for psychological treatment. Frequently we found enormous resistance to accepting the seriousness of what had taken place. The wish of both the adolescent and the parents was to forget the event as quickly as possible and to resume "normal life." This may explain why even the professional worker often responds to a suicide attempt as if what the adolescent needs at that moment is reassurance, with the belief that this can best be achieved by minimizing the seriousness of the disturbance that the suicide attempt implies. An adolescent who was in a coma for three days just before he was to write exams was encouraged to resume his studies as soon as possible so that he should not feel a total failure. The belief is that, by undoing any potential disruption of his life, the adolescent can forget about the wish to die and can go on living. When we have suggested that such an adolescent showed signs of being in urgent need of psychological help, this was often dismissed because of the implication that we did not regard him as normal or were mistaken in believing that the attempt was anything other than a reaction to some external pressure or event.

The anxiety and anger aroused in the parents, and often in the professional worker, when an adolescent attempts suicide may force them to want to convince the analyst that his view of the meaning of the suicide attempt is exaggerated. But it would be a serious error for the analyst to compromise with the assessment that the suicide attempt, whenever it took place, is a sign of the presence of severe pathology now and a risk for the adolescent's future. A suicide attempt of the past or of the present carries with it the same pathological quality. If, in the course of assessment, we learn that the adolescent had attempted suicide some time ago, "but it is not a problem now," the assessment must nevertheless be that an acute breakdown has taken place in the adolescent's life.

CLINICAL MATERIAL: Mary

The technical difficulties in Mary's analysis threatened, if unresolved, to end treatment prematurely and break off the relationship to the analyst. This crisis can be formulated as follows: the suicide attempt is relived within the transference through the compelling need to break off the analysis. The way the analyst understands and uses such crises in the transference is crucial in enabling the adolescent to experience the self-destructive impulses but without their leading to an actual breaking off of the analysis.

Treatment broke down temporarily when Mary became convinced that the analyst had turned into a frightening and angry, retaliating person who was responsible for her feeling that she was being driven mad. The patient's need to keep away from the sessions could be understood as a response to a delusion she experienced in the transference and as a psychotic defense against her perception of the analyst. In this way the psychotic aspect of the original suicide attempt was repeated in the analysis.

Mary, aged eighteen, took an overdose of antidepressants one evening and was found unconscious the next morning by her mother.[2] She was taken to the hospital and, when well enough, was transferred to a mental hospital where she remained extremely withdrawn, hesitated to eat, and spoke very little. She gave almost no clues as to why she had chosen to die. Her parents were unable to understand what had happened. They said they were aware that Mary had always been "difficult"—she was a timid and frightened child who had to be per-

2. This patient is described in a different context in chapter 7.

suaded and pushed into any new situation—but they had not thought there was anything seriously wrong. In comparision, her older brother was confident and self-assured. Mary had, however, begun to complain of feeling depressed a few weeks before the suicide attempt, and eventually her mother had taken her to the family doctor. He had arranged for her to be seen by a psychiatrist. In the meantime he had given her anti-depressants. She took these when she decided to kill herself.

When discussing the question of treatment, the analyst told Mary that she would want her to stay in the mental hospital un-til she felt Mary was well enough to leave. The analyst would then expect her to live where someone would be available to help her if she needed it.[3]

Mary was a small, slightly built girl, looking much younger than she was, with the voice and movements of an eager but timid child. She was dressed in jeans and a sweater that com-pletely covered her body, and at first she wore her coat throughout each session. Initially she was brought by her mother, who waited for her until the end of the session and then took her back to the hospital. At that time Mary said she was afraid to travel on her own. She said that she had to use clothes as a means of hiding her body. Previously in the assess-ment interviews she talked of having certain worries about her body that made her feel terrible and said that these were con-nected in some way with her wish to die. She referred to her mother's constipation; she had similar problems, and she was worried and upset by her thoughts about them. But she made it clear that she found it almost impossible to talk of these things because of the shame it made her feel. She explained that her fear of analysis was due to her inability to talk of her problems.

In the transference words took on the meaning of food in re-lation to the analyst. Then her silences were used as a way of starving the analyst. But by starving her Mary could also keep her small so that she would not become huge and able to domi-nate and control Mary. One of her chief concerns was to en-

3. See also chapter 13.

sure that she would not be made to feel "nonexistent"—this
was how she felt when she was with her mother. Her silences,
however, contained the same self-destructive meaning that she
had already demonstrated in the hospital through her determi-
nation to show that she could exist on her own without the help
or the food the hospital offered her.

She first became silent during the analysis at a time when she
was becoming increasingly anxious about what was happening
in her life outside the sessions. She needed to talk to the analyst
about it but had to deny herself the opportunity. She had at
this point left the hospital, was living away from home, and had
taken up her studies again. A conflict arose between her wish
to spend more time with a boy she had met and her need to
study. She would stay up late at night to talk to him while becoming increasingly anxious about her work and what her
teachers would do to her if she could not fulfill their require-
ments. Although she had made the decision on her own to continue her studies and write her exams, the analyst suspected
that Mary was still influenced by her fear of her mother's disapproval if she decided to end her studies.

All she could tell the analyst each day was how many hours
she had spent talking to her boyfriend—as if she were describing how she felt guilty for secretly stuffing herself with food at
night, as she had done before her suicide attempt. She was desperately anxious to prove to herself that she was normal and
could have a boyfriend, so that she did not have to fear being
left alone by her girlfriends, who she felt were more interested
in boys than in her. At the time the analyst could not fully understand all the meanings that withholding of words had for
her. She responded to interpretations as attempts to make her
talk, and this increased her compelling need to remain silent.
The analyst knew that Mary's response as "forcing her" must
be related to sexual fantasies she had of being given an enema
by someone—something she had referred to once—but at the
time she had said she hated herself for not being able to get
this thought out of her mind and that the analyst must not talk
of it to her. When she did, Mary responded angrily, saying that
the analyst made her sick by such talk. Through the analyst's

continuing to interpret her silences, she not only felt the analyst was forcing her to talk but doing something to her that made her feel "sick" and abnormal by putting the forbidden thought of the enema into her mind. Yet, responding to Mary's silence by remaining silent herself could be equally dangerous. As long as Mary could remain silent she could think that her aggression against the analyst was no longer under the analyst's control and that she had succeeded in harming her. By being silent herself the analyst could only confirm Mary's fantasy that she wished to reject Mary or that she had succeeded in "killing her" through forcing the analyst to be silent. The analyst was concerned that the anxiety this would have aroused might make Mary attempt suicide again.

While remaining silent about what was happening to her, Mary gave the analyst just sufficient information to indicate that her anxiety was threatening to overwhelm her once more. She said that she was beginning to feel as she had before her suicide attempt—everything she was doing (studying, caring for herself, coming to her sessions) was being done because she felt she had to do it. She felt herself totally dominated again. She talked of her need to be decisive and not to give in. She began to stay away from her sessions.

After she had stayed away for some days without contacting the analyst, she phoned Mary and asked her to come so that they could discuss what should be done if Mary was unable to continue with the analysis. In this way the analyst did not allow Mary to experience her as if she had been able to make the analyst "nonexistent," something she always feared that the analyst could do to her. When she came, the analyst suggested that Mary should return to the hospital because she needed help and could not use the help the analyst was able to give her. This event was the first crisis in the analysis and constituted a break in her relationship to the analyst. Through becoming active the analyst created the crisis rather than allow Mary to feel that she had destroyed her and the analysis. Once she was back in the hospital, the analyst was able to discuss with her whether she wanted to continue with her treatment. Mary could now be confronted with her anger with the analyst, knowing that she felt safer to decide because she did not have to feel totally dependent on the analyst to help her. The analyst could show her how her staying away had been an attack on herself and her hopes about her future life as well as on the analyst. She could also help Mary understand that she would have felt driven to want to kill herself had the analyst not contacted her because she would have felt alone and hopeless once more.

Later Mary explained that she had not come because she had felt so violent that she thought she would destroy the analyst's room if she came, and that when she did come she had felt constantly frightened of her—as if the analyst was going to attack her. In fact, when she had decided to stay away from her sessions, she had become so fearful at night that she had asked to sleep in the room of the woman who looked after the house she lived in. During the day she had not been able to leave the house. Her inability to contact the analyst was determined by her paranoid fantasy of the analyst's dominating her and forcing her to have shaming thoughts that would make her sick and abnormal and want to kill herself. But Mary's only means of defense was by attacking the analyst and making her "nonexistent" in her life by her insistence that she had to manage without her help. Through the analyst's acknowledgment of the reality of Mary's attack on her by confronting her with the analyst's inability to help, while at the same time insisting on her need for help, Mary could experience her own destructive impulses without feeling totally alone and abandoned by the analyst. It was important, technically, to acknowledge the effect of Mary's actions for the analyst to avoid presenting herself as an omnipotent object who could continue to be attacked. At the same time the analyst acknowledged the compelling nature of the attack, and thus the severity of her illness.

Mary herself had always dismissed attaching any significance to the timing of her suicide attempt. She had already felt dead, she said, for the previous two years, so there was nothing special about why she had chosen that day. But the analyst's assumption that they had worked through a crucial aspect of Mary's motivation for wanting to kill herself was confirmed some time later by an incident that the analyst took as an indication that Mary was no longer as vulnerable to reacting to her anxiety in the same way. She had been home for a weekend and reported that she became angry with her parents because, although they had not openly quarreled, there had been "an atmosphere" in the home—a hostile silence between the parents. She had told them that she did not want to spend time with them if that was all they could do. Then, to "relieve her feelings," she had gone for a long walk before returning home. She remembered that the evening before she took the overdose there had been a similar atmosphere, and she had gone to bed early to get away from it. This was evidence that she was now able to express her own feelings more directly and did not have to feel so helpless or experience her own feelings as if they were nonexistent and only the result of what her parents were doing to her.

Much of her material about her parents had concerned itself with her mixture of triumph and anxiety about her parents' relationship. She felt that her father could talk to her but could not or would not talk to her mother. Thus, talking had an oedipal significance, and her guilt about damaging her mother contained her belief that talking to her father damaged her mother because it kept him from talking to her mother. This event further confirmed Mary's feeling that talking to her boyfriend and being silent with the analyst was an attack on the analyst and that Mary's inability to come to the sessions was partly her fear of the analyst's retaliation.

The period of analysis before the temporary interruption in treatment can also be seen as a repetition of the two years preceding Mary's suicide attempt when she felt she had given up and when secretly she knew that she could kill herself. At that time, she felt she had to allow her life to be controlled more and more by her mother. She felt preoccupied with her mother's constipation, and this interest in her mother's body was represented in the paranoid fantasy where she experienced her mother as the source of her sexual fantasies. But in identifying her mother as the source of these fantasies that had made her so "sick" with herself and tormented her so much, she was left feeling that she could either give in to her mother and to her own thoughts or destroy her mother to rid herself of them. She showed the strength of her belief that her mother was responsible for her thoughts when she mentioned having been convinced once or twice that her mother was offering her food that was poisoned. But it was when she was alone and trying to study for her examinations that her illness had become acute, and she had broken down. She had become unable to concentrate on her studies or to control the thoughts about her body. She told the analyst how she had felt during that time of getting food secretly and stuffing herself during the night. She could no longer avoid feeling responsible for her own thoughts and impulses and instead hated herself for making herself fat—as if she felt her body was responsible for exposing her shameful secret.

When she had been staying up late at night with the young man she had met, talking had increasingly given way to touching, and these feelings made her extremely anxious. She would mention that they had talked until 3 in the morning but gave no other details. The technical problem at first was to decide how much of her wish to keep her new relationship secret represented an attempt at a progressive move away from feeling controlled by her mother and now by the analyst and how much anxiety it left her to deal with on her own because she was unable to allow the analyst to help her. During the first week of her new friendship, Mary talked in a panic of feeling afraid of losing control and saying that she had thought of suicide the day before. Suicide was her "only lifeline." She said she had been aware of being "completely at his mercy," that they had kissed and cuddled. It was as if she saw suicide as her only escape to remain in control. What later seemed the first danger signal, despite interpretations to help her talk of her anxiety and guilt, was that Mary still felt compelled to go home and talk to her mother about what had happened. Although she claimed to have felt better after doing so, she phoned the analyst in a panic the same evening and asked to come for an extra session. She then told the analyst how guilty she had felt because she had been unable to tell the analyst that the young man had touched her genitals.

This evidence of Mary's compulsive need to tell her mother in order to get relief from her guilt, and her anxiety about her silence with the analyst, contributed to the analyst's concern about Mary's continuing inability to talk in the sessions. Despite interpretations it was evident that the analyst was unable to prevent Mary's mounting anxiety about the material she was withholding, which at the same time made her see the analyst as helpless.

Mary remained in the hospital for the next five months. During this time she began to be able to be more friendly with the other patients, and she could respond to the staff's therapeutic interventions much more constructively. Initially, she rejected all help or relationships other than those that she sought out to protect herself from the aggression and violence she felt surrounded her. But gradually she could begin to acknowledge her own aggressive and sexual fantasies. She realized that she not only did not want to study and write exams but would like to feel able to work and earn money so that she did not have to feel so helpless and dependent. Later, she expressed her pleasure at finding how much freer she now felt by saying that she had never realized that one could eat when one was hungry instead of having to eat at certain times only.

The second time Mary apparently decided to end her treatment occurred a year later, when she had begun to work. She was extremely anxious that nobody should know of her need for treatment and tried to conceal her past psychiatric admissions as well as her present need for help. When her employer asked for a medical history, she became intensely anxious and aggressive. The problem became part of the tranference when she was unable to come to her sessions on time because of demands at work. She could not tell her employer that she needed to leave, nor could she tell the analyst why she was late or why she had not come the previous day. She used the analyst to show that no one could make her explain her behavior if she did not want to.

She decided that she would only continue analysis four times a week instead of five. It was becoming "too much" for her. Again she tried to use her "decisiveness" as a means of feeling in control. But her fear of losing control was that she would be forced to reveal her shameful secrets. The analyst insisted that Mary needed five sessions and interpreted her behavior of staying away, not telling the analyst why she was late when she did come, and silence about the life outside the treatment as the wish to remain in control because of her fear of losing control of her anger with the analyst. She became increasingly angry, and her behavior toward the analyst did not seem to change as the result of interpretations. She came late, refused to speak, and left the analyst quite unaware of why she could not come. She had begun to make friends, and at times it seemed that it was not her work that kept her from attending but rather her wish to spend time with them. When she demanded to cut down her sessions, the analyst said that she saw Mary's uncertainty about the use of treatment and its being "too much" as her feeling that the analyst was now somebody she had to avoid. She suggested that Mary should think about whether she wanted to continue.

The analyst asked her to sit up so that they could discuss why the analyst believed that Mary still needed to come despite her present ability to manage. After some days they agreed that Mary needed some time to think it over. On the last day of the agreed period she phoned to say that she had decided to stop her analysis. Two days later she called in a state of panic asking the analyst whether she had already acted in response to Mary's decision to end analysis and saying that she wanted to see the analyst because she felt she had made one of her terrible mistakes.

When she returned, she said that when she had called to tell the analyst of her decision she had intended to say that she wanted to continue, but at the last moment a friend who was in some distress had asked to talk to her, and she had impulsively changed her mind, saying she would not continue. It was as if the friend had enabled her temporarily to feel identified with the omnipotent analyst so that she could feel as if she had no needs herself. Only after she had told the analyst she would not continue, had she really been able to experience what ending her analysis would mean to her. She had spent a dreadful two days—she felt as if she had come to a full stop before she could decide to phone the analyst to ask whether she could still continue. It seemed as if she was repeating something that was clear earlier in the analysis. At the time of taking the overdose she had been unable to think of death in real terms. While she was in the hospital, however, a patient she knew had died as the result of an overdose, and only then could Mary feel frightened of death and relieved that she had not died. Her need to experience what it was like to end analysis before being able to feel what it meant to her to lose the analyst and the treatment seemed to repeat this same denial of reality.

From a technical point of view it had been important to stand firm in the face of Mary's demand that the analyst protect her from things in her life becoming "too much" for her. Had the analyst allowed her to miss the sessions, it would have meant that she agreed that Mary should not be exposed to any situation that caused her too much anxiety. It would also have meant that the analyst agreed with and accepted Mary's fear of losing control of her anger, which for her would have included not only the analyst or people at work but also any future sexual relationships. By showing her how she was still vulnerable to dealing with her anxiety by the need to break off the relationship with the analyst, Mary could be given back the hope that analysis could enable her to maintain a stable relationship in the future. Experiencing the need to break off the analysis repeated her suicidal impulse, and this enabled her to experience her self-destructive impulse within the safety of the transference relationship.[4]

---

4. Since this case was part of a research study, it was discussed at regular clinical research meetings with colleagues who were also treating adolescents. We soon became aware that these discussions were essential as a support when treating adolescents where the possibility of another suicide attempt had always to be kept in mind.

III
CLINICAL ISSUES

9
Compulsive Behavior and the Central Masturbation Fantasy: Clinical Implications

In our psychoanalytic treatment of adolescents we have frequently been faced with the need to deal with specific actions or acting-out behaviors that have endangered patients' lives or have at least placed them in serious danger of harming themselves—for example, extensive drug taking, attempted suicide, becoming pregnant, or actions that could result in legal proceedings with consequences such as imprisonment or compulsory admission to a psychiatric hospital. Colleagues who treat adolescents psychoanalytically have confirmed that such behaviors are not at all uncommon during the treatment of seriously disturbed adolescents. In certain circumstances, they may mean that the psychoanalyst must do something about the behavior lest the adolescent actually be endangered. In less serious circumstances, the treatment may end as the result of certain actions.

We hesitate to discuss some of the technical issues encountered in the treatment of such seriously disturbed adolescents for fear of creating the false impression that "management" of one kind or another is sufficient to overcome some of the very difficult problems with which the analyst is faced. Many adolescents in treatment are in the midst of a serious crisis in their lives, often with the need to make decisions affecting their future education and work. Sometimes, concern about an immediate crisis is mistakenly seen as a resistance, and the unconscious significance of the crisis can be lost. Although temporary

135

adaptation of classical technique is appropriate in dealing with such crises in an adolescent's life, a mere change of technique is rarely sufficient to overcome such problems in our day-to-day work (Eissler 1958; Geleerd 1957; Harley 1970). It is more likely that the repeated limitations of our psychoanalytic technique represent our limited knowledge about the structure of the psychopathologies of adolescence (A. Freud 1958; Harley 1961). These limitations may keep us out of touch with the meaning of the adolescent's anxiety and with the immediate internal factors that contribute to a picture of disorganization and being out of control.

Some adolescent patients share a characteristic which is an indication that it may be necessary for the analyst to intervene in the adolescent's behavior. In the course of the analysis, and often early in the therapeutic contact, it becomes clear that the adolescent is not able to stop himself from doing certain serious and sometimes dangerous things. *This compulsive behavior is equivalent to the repetitive living out in the outside world of a specific fantasy or fantasies.* It also becomes clear that the more he lives out these fantasies, the more anxious and disorganized he seems to become. As treatment progresses, the patient begins to acknowledge that interpretation of the meaning of the specific fantasy or fantasies does not help him to stop putting them into action. But the dilemma is that the success or failure of treatment may depend precisely on this ability to isolate these fantasies and bring them into the analysis for understanding and working through. Reality factors, such as the real danger to the patient of some of his actions, do not seem to have any impact on him. In such circumstances, it becomes important for the analyst temporarily to place clearly defined limits on the adolescent's behavior. The analyst must then, through intervention, bring this material into the treatment. However, such an intervention must never be simply an external matter imposed by the analyst; it must be something that is understood by the patient as being necessary and of potential help to the progress of the treatment. Such intervention took place during Jane's treatment, described in this chapter.

The timing of the intervention is crucial. We do not think it would be of any use if it was brought into the treatment before the adolescent felt he had a relationship to the analyst. It is important to wait until he acknowledges that his pathology and behavior are interfering seriously with his life—when he begins to see that his need for certain forms of action or acting out is a serious problem in his life. It would be an error to intervene unless the intervention can make emotional sense to the adolescent. It must therefore come at a time when the adolescent can allow himself to use the analyst temporarily as an auxiliary ego or auxiliary superego.

One danger in intervening, of course, is that the treatment may then become sexualized: the adolescent may feel that he has been able to force the analyst to become the controlling and punishing superego and that, in this way, he is forcing the analyst to fit into his fantasy of being passively subdued by the analyst. The sexualization of the treatment can be a very serious resistance, but it is nevertheless more manageable than the continuous loss of the content of the fantasy through the adolescent's actions outside the sessions, as well as the loss of the affect attached to these actions.

The adolescents we refer to are usually very vulnerable people, some with histories of attempted suicide, self-mutilation, extensive drug taking, or promiscuity. Because of their vulnerability, the analyst may hesitate to disturb the treatment and may want to avoid any unnecessary crises, especially if they have previously attempted suicide. Some of these adolescents unconsciously know that their vulnerability frightens people and makes them kind and cautious toward them. The analyst may also tend to try to avoid the adolescent's negative transference reactions, partly in the belief that taking up the negative transference might provoke the patient to break off treatment or to act out in some other way. But such avoidance by the analyst produces greater anxiety in the adolescent because he will unconsciously sense that the analyst, too, is frightened. This itself results in a greater need on the part of the adolescent to act out this aspect of the transference. Acting out can then become confused in the adolescent's mind with other forms of uncontrolled behavior, and he will become even more frightened by his actions (Blos 1966; A. Freud 1968; Limentani 1966; Rosenfeld 1964).

The adolescents to whom we are referring feel temporarily unable to stop some of their behavior without the analyst's help—a feeling that exists well before treatment has begun. The treatment may highlight the adolescent's need to repeat certain forms of behavior that are in fact part of the pathology, but the treatment itself does not produce the need to repeat the behavior. Perhaps only after the analyst places defined limits on some specific behavior may the adolescent feel able to gain some insight into the meaning of the fantasies that compel him to behave in certain ways. With some adolescents we have treated by psychoanalysis, treatment begins to get under way only after these fantasies are "pulled" into the analysis. Once these actions come under analytic scrutiny, it becomes obvious that the fantasies that these adolescents are compelled to live out in a repetitive way are their central masturbation fantasy.

Except for this intervention in a very clearly defined area of the patients' lives, it is essential to use classical analytic technique. Unnecessary intervention confuses the adolescent and distorts the development of the transference by making it impossible for him to differentiate between behavior that he feels compelled to live out and behavior that is specifically related to the treatment and to the present state of the transference.

CLINICAL MATERIAL: Jane

Jane was seen irregularly from the ages of fourteen to seventeen and then in psychoanalytic treatment to the age of twenty-four.[1] When Jane was first brought by her parents, she was attending a school in another city. The analyst arranged to see her irregularly because of the distance involved, but he was concerned from the start because of her general manner. She always smiled and seemed especially polite and understanding. Her parents had been worried about her isolation, her depression, and her unpredictable moods. They had separated five

1. This patient is also referred to in chapter 2.

years earlier but kept in contact with each other about Jane's behavior and about their concern for her unhappiness.

When it was time for Jane to decide about her further education, she said she was thinking of applying to a university outside of London so that she could "get away from everything." By this time she knew that the analyst took a serious view of her disturbance. He said he thought she should have intensive treatment and therefore suggested that she apply to a college in London. She knew there were no analysts in the city where she was attending school. She did not decide about this for some months, saying that she could not be sure whether intensive treatment would help or destroy her. During this period of his contact with Jane, he did not know what this fear really referred to and therefore felt that it would be sufficient simply to say that he was worried about her and that she needed to have treatment. Only much later in her analysis could the analyst make sense of her fear of being destroyed and of her wish to get the analyst to take over the responsibility for this decision. She finally decided to apply to a nearby university so that intensive treatment could be undertaken.

Jane was actually eager and relieved to be able to come to treatment on a regular basis. She had become very frightened at school when she had what she described as a "hysterical attack" on a school outing—crying, shouting, demanding to be taken back to the school. She was worried about being "sexually abnormal," which to her meant that she might be a lesbian; she was unable to have any close relationships with boys; and she felt compelled to masturbate ("the little man in me tells me to do it, and it is as if I just have to").

Jane attempted suicide seven months after her analysis began. She had been going out with Bill, aged twenty-five, whom she described as a depressed, ineffectual person who behaved as if he was grateful to her for allowing him to be her boyfriend. They had intercourse regularly, but Jane was never able to have a climax. This was a constant source of worry to her, making her feel that it was a confirmation of her abnormality. More specifically, it seemed to the analyst that she was repeatedly being faced with her preference for masturbation,

when she could experience in fantasy the idea of being humiliated, overwhelmed, and sometimes raped.

Before she started her relationship with Bill, Jane had been
promiscuous for about a year. She would have intercourse with
men in a rather indiscriminate way and then would hate herself for this, saying that she was just a "slut" and "should be
dead." But intercourse never did what she hoped it would, and
she began to masturbate in a rather compulsive way. The effort
at that point in the analysis to understand the fantasy during
masturbation was not at all successful; only later the analyst
learned about the part of the fantasy she never described when
she talked about masturbation. She told him that she would
imagine in masturbation that somebody (she was not sure who)
was masturbating her furiously and that the only important
thing was that she have a climax. The masturbation was often
preceded by eating, drinking, or by reading a romantic novel.

The guilt Jane experienced as the result of her masturbation
was such that she found it extremely difficult to do her college
work or to concentrate on anything other than the most mun-
dane chores. She felt completely paralyzed by the need to try to
disprove her abnormality; everything else took second place.
But she was referring to something related to the treatment
and to a limitation the analyst had placed on her behavior a
short time after her analysis had begun. It was this specific limitation that made it possible for her to be confronted with the
masturbation fantasy and with the fact that she had to live it
out in a compelling way. The behavior that the analyst wanted
to limit was this: When Jane was at school in another city,
sometimes she would hitchhike into London. An attractive girl,
she was often given a ride by someone who then asked for her
telephone number or tried to pet or have intercourse with her.
She never permitted intercourse with any of these men, but she
would often allow them to become sexually aroused through
petting. A number of times she was given rides by men who
threatened to beat her up or to harm her in some other way.
The analyst became very concerned because her behavior had
a compelling quality and because in reality she was placing herself in serious danger.

By this time the analyst realized that Jane was living out her central masturbation fantasy through her hitchhiking. The compelling quality of her hitchhiking gave him the clue that the core of her pathology was contained in the fantasy that was being lived out. The analyst had tried many times previously to convey to her some of the meaning of the hitchhiking, but she invariably had found reasons to "accept" an offer of a ride. She had, by then, begun to recognize that she could not give this activity up, but she denied any anxiety about it. The analyst told her that, for some unknown reason, she could not give up hitchhiking and that he was very concerned for her safety. He also said that, unless she stopped hitchhiking, they would not be able to understand what was forcing her to behave in this way, thus interfering with the treatment. He added: "It is for this reason that I think you should not hitchhike any longer." Jane was both furious and relieved. He was aware that such a decision might interfere with the normal course of the treatment, but he felt that they had reached a point in the analysis where Jane could see that she could not stop this behavior on her own.

The central masturbation fantasy was the following:

> She is being chased, and is then caught, by a man who looks completely unconcerned and has no feelings at all. This man then gets her to do all kinds of things for him in a slavelike way and then proceeds to arouse her sexually. He is in complete control of himself and of what is going on. She submits to his demands for sexual activity, but the fantasy ends abruptly just before they have intercourse.[2]

Although this was her central masturbation fantasy, in fact in masturbation she did not consciously have this fantasy. It was usually lived out in some way in her relationship with people, as for example, in the hitchhiking. The fantasy during masturbation was much more neutral and, as she said, much more "clinical"—that is, she did it "just to get physical relief."

Jane constantly complained of her relationship with Bill, say-

2. Toward the latter part of the treatment, there was further elaboration of this fantasy. See chapter 2.

ing that he humiliated himself in her eyes, that he was not strong enough, and that she could get him to do anything she asked. In the transference, she continually tried to put the analyst into the position of the man in her masturbation fantasy by insisting that he show his strength and by saying that he did not care for her if he only talked and did not take any active part in stopping her from doing things. On Mondays she would describe her weekend behavior with Bill, demanding that the analyst do something to control her and saying that he was stupid to go on treating her. Why did he not stop treatment? She was no good, worthless, dirty, and he was no better if he listened to her and allowed her to come to see him each day. (When the analyst had decided earlier to stop the hitch-hiking, he was concerned that he might fit into her fantasy of being the brutal, cold person who forced her to submit to him. But the reality was such that he felt he must take that chance and bring the ensuing transference factor into the treatment.)

Up to the time preceding her suicide attempt, Jane and the analyst had recognized Jane's fear of her abnormality, her worry about being a lesbian, her belief that she had in some way been responsible for her parents' separation, and her great discomfort in being with other people of her own age. Masturbation, she felt convinced, confirmed that there was something seriously wrong with her mentally, but at the same time she felt unable to "forget about it, or at least not have to go on doing it." These problems were discussed at great length in treatment. But any mention by the analyst of her wish for him to declare his love for her or any reference to the extent of the destructive capacity she felt she had inside herself were completely rejected—to the point where she told him that he was accusing her of "thinking about things which don't exist," that he did not really show interest in her, and that she sometimes wanted to run away and die. While in the sessions she often talked in a very quiet voice, smiled in a rather waxlike way, and held tightly to her feelings. But outside the sessions, she often argued with her boyfriend, cried and screamed, would not talk for hours at a time, and occasionally would stay in her room and not allow anyone to come in.

Two weeks before her suicide attempt, she became extremely anxious about her repeated masturbation. She continued to have intercourse with Bill but complained that it was all useless, that she did not feel that intercourse satisfied her but at the same time could not give it up. If she did, she would be left on her own and to herself, and she would just go on trying to excite herself, and that would be terrible and abnormal. Interpretation at this point did not seem to have any effect. She became increasingly agitated and said that she just could not stop masturbating, a factor that could have been used to predict that a severe crisis was imminent.

At college, she met an older woman student, and they became friendly. This woman obligingly told Jane that masturbation was a very good way of ridding oneself of tension, and Jane took this remark as permission to go on masturbating. The result, however, was not temporary relief but much greater anxiety and a feeling that she was now free to lose complete control of herself. To Jane, this simply exaggerated the extent to which she felt that her body was her enemy and that one way to rid herself of that dirty, horrible thing that made her feel lesbian was to kill it. When this older woman friend (who represented Jane's relationship to her lonely and isolated mother) told Jane to masturbate, Jane felt excited by this kind of closeness. Interpretation of her wish for closeness to this woman and to her mother made her silent and frightened. She accused the analyst of not caring because he had not tried to stop her masturbation.

The day before the suicide attempt, Jane came to her session saying that she felt she was losing control of herself and that suddenly everything had gone out of her life. She giggled when she said she had thought of hitchhiking "somewhere." The analyst tried to get to what he thought was now the core of her anxiety—that is, that she regarded her thoughts as very abnormal and was ashamed of what she felt and thought. When he referred to the "little man in her who tells her to do it," she simply said that she could not talk about "certain things." (Some months after her suicide attempt she was able then to talk about a part of her thoughts that nobody must take

away from her. She did not know what this was, but she felt
there was a part of her mind that nobody could or would get
to; it was hers, and she could not give that part away.)

Jane was alone at home when she took an overdose of pills.
Her boyfriend found her some hours later. It was two days before she fully regained consciousness in the hospital. The analyst visited her there once for an analytic session, after which
she came on her own, or was brought, to her sessions from the
hospital. She stayed in the hospital for five months, during
which she was very difficult, often sullen, argued with the
other patients, sometimes broke dishes, and once disappeared
for several hours before she was found sitting by the bank of a
river. When asked by the nurse why she had stormed out of
the hospital (something she did on two occasions in treatment),
Jane said that she had had an argument with another girl in
the ward and felt that one way of settling it all was to jump into
the river. She became involved in fights in the ward, slapped
some of the male patients who "keep on trying to touch me,"
and was generally unpredictable and extremely moody.

Her sessions during the period following her suicide attempt
were almost totally disorganized. Interpretation of her defensive behavior in relation to her fear that she was abnormal or to
her worry that she might really kill herself or to her fear that
she would attack her mother helped only slightly. She remained extremely anxious, and in general there was little
change. She often cried in her sessions, pulled at her hair, and
said repeatedly, "I *must* die. It will never be right. I must die."
She felt nothing would be right until she did die. The analyst
decided that he had to make his position clear to her at this
point—that is, that he was in reality not able to stop her from
killing herself. He felt now that, whatever the interpretation of
her present behavior might be, it was equally important to
bring reality into the treatment. He explained that he could
help her, but only if she felt she wanted to go on living. If she
wanted to kill herself, he could not stop her, and he reminded
her that her wish to die and her earlier suicide attempt were
signs of illness. He could help her with her illness, but only if
she had decided that she wanted help. She was furious, but at
the same time she seemed to calm down.

From this time, Jane began to talk about feeling that she was going completely mad and was on the verge of what she described as "disintegration." She could not describe it in any other way, she said. She felt terrified of that "core" to which she had referred earlier in treatment, and which she felt she could not let anyone get to. She repeated often that her feeling of going mad was in this core of her thinking, which she had never been able to share with anyone. The trouble was, she said, that she did not really know what this core was all about. She felt that she was dirty and useless, that she just had to die. Nothing else could take the place of death.

At this juncture the analyst reminded Jane of an incident that she could not mention and that she felt she must somehow eliminate from her body. Soon after her treatment began, she had met a man who had taken her to his home. There he masturbated her with a tubelike object. She had felt completely crazy when this happened—she had enjoyed it and felt disgusted by it. She was convinced that it was only through death that she could purge this experience "from my body." Death was the only way this experience could be "ended once and for all." Then all the secrets would be dead, too. But she could not define these secrets—she did not know what they were, but she felt they were always there to be hidden from herself as well as from others.

Jane then described how terrified she had been of treatment—that is, of finding out that she was irreversibly abnormal. She could not tell the analyst things freely because this would mean that she had given in to him. And if she gave in to him, "then it means that I will have to tell you that I care. People think that things don't matter to me, that I'm cold, or that I'm satisfied with everything." She suddenly became silent. Before the end of that session, she began to cry and could then say that she was convinced the analyst would not be able to help her. She could not be sure whether he liked her or despised her; whatever she did, it did not seem to frighten him. She felt safe because of this, but at the same time he might despise her for her behavior. In fact, she was referring to some of her recent behavior in the hospital—fighting with the other patients, drinking wine and "making myself stupid," and spending much time with a young married woman (also a patient) who had violent outbursts of anger.

The crisis seemed very serious at that point, and the analyst was unsure about Jane's prognosis or, for that matter, about her day-to-day behavior. He felt that, technically, it was important not to try to use reconstruction but instead to make conscious some of the content of her daydreams in order to link it to her other extreme behavior. It seemed to him that reconstruction at this moment in the crisis might temporarily alleviate the anxiety but, on the other hand, might also produce greater anxiety because it would not help her feel more able to control her behavior. He tried, therefore, to concentrate on the details of her behavior in hospital: when she went to sleep, what she ate, how she spent her day, what she thought about while in the ward, what she read, whom she talked to, and so on. From these details he could begin to understand the extent to which Jane felt bewildered by what had gone on recently in her life and the extent to which she felt that she could lose control at any time.

One day she began her session by saying that she had again thought "I must die." She felt she must talk to the analyst about it. On the bus on the way to the session, she had felt crazy again. In the waiting room, she did not know what to do—should she sit or stand, read, look out of the window? Nothing had felt right. She had to do something. She thought it would be nice to tear the analyst's skin with her fingernails, or maybe she should do it to somebody else. The analyst was so detached, and all he wanted to do was understand; maybe tearing his skin would break him down. She then felt very frightened. She pulled at her hair and began to scream, saying, "I don't know what it is. I really must die. Please help me."

She reacted with astonishment when she remembered that she had awakened during the night from a nightmare. She had completely forgotten about this; it just came back. She could not recall the details, but it felt horrible. Now she felt crazy. The nightmare made her feel crazy. She remembered the following dream: Jane is being loved by, and is loving, another girl. She thought it would be nice to masturbate this girl and to be masturbated by her. She couldn't remember anything else about this nightmare except that the nurse woke her up while she was dreaming. She had felt terrible. She had not been able to fall asleep for a long time because of the thoughts about this girl. When she awoke, she did not remember the dream at all. She went on feeling terrible and thinking that she must die, that there was no hope, that she was no good, and that she would never get out of hospital.

Jane recalled that on the previous evening she had felt very miserable. The ward had seemed very depressing. She had gone out and had bought some wine, even though she knew that the hospital prohibited this. She and another patient (the young married woman) had begun to drink the wine. As she drank, she had felt a sensation in her vagina, as if she wanted something to happen. She thought how nice it might be to touch this other patient, to hold her and perhaps to be loved by her. "I love and I hate her. When I was getting drunk, I wanted her to hold me and I wanted to hold her." The dream was awful. It made her feel hopeless and dangerous.

She remembered how she and her sister (who was one year younger) used to sleep in the same room as children. Sometimes they would sleep in the same bed, and when it was dark they would even hold each other. Sometimes, as little children, they would "tell" each other when to start masturbating. This meant that they had a word that meant that one had started to masturbate, and this then meant that the other would start. When Bill had intercourse with her, he didn't seem to know that what she really wanted was to be held—just held and made safe, nothing else. She used to hate intercourse because it reminded her that she was abnormal; she couldn't have a climax, and she felt so dirty all the time. That would never change. But she had to go on having intercourse because otherwise she would just want to be with girls, and that would make her want to die. When her father had visited her in the hospital the other day, all she had been able to do was cry. She liked him less now than she used to, and she didn't know whether she blamed him for what she did. It was so confusing; she felt so abnormal and so lonely, and she did not know whether it would help to blame anybody. But at the same time, when she thought of dying, she sometimes thought that she could in this way make others feel that it was their fault. But that wasn't the real reason for wanting to die. It was because she had to get rid of all those secrets in her body.

When the analyst said that it seemed from the dream as if she preferred to be held rather than have intercourse and that this feeling of wanting to be held was for her a proof of her abnormality, she recalled how she had wanted to touch the woman patient the previous night. She "almost did it, but I don't know what made me stop." When the analyst said that her bewilderment and her feeling that she must die were partially her way of punishing her body for wanting such things and that it was as if she really now wanted to be held by her mother, Jane replied that when she was "coming round after I took the overdose, my mother was sitting by my bed. My mother told me that I said to her that she and I were closer to each other now than ever before. I hated her for telling me that. And I forgot it until now." But now she felt as if she could fight this just a little. Maybe she didn't have to be lesbian; maybe it was more that she hated Bill for being weak and so dependent. Her father had once cried when he and her mother were thinking of separating, and Jane had hated him too. But when he left, she felt as if she herself had driven him out of the house; it was as if she wanted to be alone with her mother, but at the same time she knew that her father was now strong.

She hated the analyst too for being strong, but she also didn't hate him. When he came to the hospital to see her, she remembered thinking that he might look frightened, but he didn't. "I thought you might be angry with me for letting you down. But I remember that you said you couldn't stop me from killing myself if I wanted to. It felt as if you were telling me to die. But I knew what you meant. Will I get you to throw me out? How can you take this from me? Why don't you do what you should? You should say you don't want to see me any more." When the analyst answered that she needed him now to confirm for her the feeling that she was worthless and that she could drive him away as she felt she had driven her father away, she did not reply. She was silent for the few remaining minutes of the session. When she left, she was crying. As she walked out of the consulting room, she said, "I'll be all right. Don't worry."

The analyst had previously interpreted Jane's attachment to her sister as representing her wish to be close to her mother and to be held by her. But Jane had said that she never felt this "even though it sounds right." This dream seemed to enable her to begin to bring material which was related to her "secrets" and to her feeling that there was a "core" that nobody, not even herself, could get to. But she also now spent a great deal of time being silent. Sometimes she would leave at the end of a session feeling very angry; at other times she would smile and say goodbye. Her silences showed the extent of her fear that the analyst might break her down and also her feeling that she could at times come to a session and be left alone with him without having to be the "best patient." After she had understood part of the dream, she felt that it was less necessary to say "I must die." She now changed this to: "I think I should die." She said that if she were "really mad," or if she "might be mad" in the future, it would be better to be dead. She had seen some of the more ill patients, and they were so miserable. What was the purpose of living like that? She might as well finish it off, and everybody, including the analyst, might be relieved. At the same time, she felt slightly more hopeful. It was as if the dream had devastated her, but it hadn't really, and that made her more hopeful. But she felt frightened when she went to bed because she might have another dream like that. She asked the ward doctor for sleeping pills, which she said were her way of making sure that she was not awakened by something from inside attacking her as it did in the dream.

For weeks Jane was unable to fall asleep even after taking the sleeping pills. The analyst concentrated during this time on her feeling that she would be overwhelmed by her inside attacker and by the abnormal part of herself. This seemed to help. She began to ask during her sessions whether it might be a good idea to "risk" going to bed without taking the pills. At this point, he did not interpret the obvious transference meaning that she felt more trust in him and that he was now helping her. When she began to take fewer sleeping pills, she sometimes spent part of the night awake and thinking that she must not give in to the abnormal part of herself. She risked having "horrible dreams" because she thought that these would help them understand the "crazy part" of her. But she remained frightened because she thought that if she did not sleep she would then have to go on masturbating, and that would be "the end."

After approximately six weeks in the hospital, Jane felt able to return to the university for part of each day. At first she felt ashamed of being ill. She thought of leaving the university and finding work "where I can be away from normal people." But she felt relieved and less vulnerable when she became friendly with another female student who herself had thought of suicide and who was now very depressed and unable to keep up with her studies. Soon after her return to the university, Jane "suddenly found that I could tell Bill I didn't want him." It was as if she could give him up and, if necessary, risk "going back to masturbating all the time." To her this meant that she was running the risk of becoming seriously ill again. She was also worried that she might want to start hitchhiking again and perhaps get a man to do something to her—that is, to harm her in some way. This was her constant daydream—of being chased, caught, overpowered, and humiliated in some way. She said she knew that she had agreed not to hitchhike.

Jane brought her daydreams now into the transference through her lengthy silences and her refusal to tell the analyst what she was thinking about. At first this made her anxious and very angry. When he interpreted her present silence as equivalent to getting him to run after her, catch her, and force her to talk—that is, of her wanting to satisfy the wish in the daydream here in the session—she could admit that "when I am silent I sometimes feel excited, and I wait for you to force me." The rape fantasy was obvious, and when he said that she wanted him forcibly to get into her, she said it was just this fantasy that had made her feel most excited sexually in her rela-

tionship with Bill. She used to walk around in the nude in front
of her father, hoping that she could get him excited so that he
would do something to her. She remembered how, when her
parents separated, she used to visit her father. Once when she
stayed the weekend with him, she got into his bed in the nude
and slept near him. She hoped he would do something to her,
but when he told her to put on some clothes, she felt despair
and thought then that "everything was hopeless." She used to
try to "fool him in all kinds of ways": she would leave the bath-
room door unlocked or would call to him when she was having
a bath, but it did not work. He never gave in. Jane's silences in
her sessions contained this theme of fooling the analyst, of
withholding things that she felt he should know, or of talking
in generalizations so that he would not be sure what she meant.
To her, fooling him was equivalent now to having a secret, a
"core that nobody could get to."

After Jane had been out of the hospital for nearly six
months, she met Jim, a student, who quickly became her boyfriend. Until then she had spent a great deal of time alone. Jim
knew that she had attempted suicide. He felt that her illness
was now past and thought there was no need for her to continue with her daily treatment. She told the analyst of this and
said that she, too, had thought of coming less often but was
afraid to give the analyst up because he was the only person
who was not afraid of her and also kept her "in control." She
was sure that she would "go wild again if I stop coming here."
During those times when she was getting along well with her
boyfriend, she was able to talk to the analyst about what was
going on and how she felt, and together they seemed able to
continue to try to understand Jane's feeling that she must die.
If she argued with Jim or felt that the analyst did not like her,
she would say that she was again thinking of suicide. He interpreted the threat, the feeling of hopelessness, the attack on her
body, or the attack on the internalized parent. But aside from
actual interpretations, he made it clear that he could not stop
her. She had become familiar now with the probability that
her thoughts about killing herself were brought on by some
thought or action that she considered to be a sign of abnormal-

ity. When she could tell the analyst about the fellatio-cunni-lingus between herself and Jim she could again stop threatening to kill herself.

The recognition that her anxiety about abnormality and the thought that she must die were linked to a thought or action that she considered abnormal was an important insight. It also helped her to withstand some of the pressure from her boyfriend to attend her sessions less often. She said, "It feels a bit untrue that maybe something can change." In some ways, it felt safer to be ill—then everybody could say, "She's not well, don't be angry with her." Her parents had had trouble in the past; sometimes she even wondered whether there might be something wrong with her mother. She remembered that her mother had told her about two or three years ago to "have a go," that is, to feel free to masturbate when she felt tense. Jane then wondered at times whether her mother really wanted to force her to masturbate. "Permission is all right, but does she know what she is saying when she says such a thing?"

Within this context the analyst's earlier request that she stop hitchhiking could again be brought into the treatment. She had previously mentioned her wish to hitchhike "just for the fun of it," but she was able to stop herself from doing this. Now she wanted to try again to see if she could be in control of what might occur. When she said this and the analyst did not immediately reply, she asked why he did not care any longer. What had she done? What was the use then? Why get better if it didn't matter to him? Here he made the link again with part of her daydream: of feeling forced to do certain things, of being chased, and now of wanting again to try to get the analyst to show her that he was the one in control, but at the same time the one who was detached. He also said that she knew now that she did not have to hitchhike, she had the control. What was important for her now was for him to show that he wanted her to be loyal only to him—that is, to keep her body only for him. She reacted to this by being silent, and then began to cry. He said nothing when she cried. Before she left she said, "When you said that, you took it away from me [referring to her feeling that, in the analyst knowing her secret source of gratification, she would no longer experience it as pleasurable]. Now I feel you don't want me."

The next day Jane arrived saying, "I'm sorry about yesterday. I didn't want to be upset, and I didn't want to upset you. It was only a bit of a shock to hear you say what I've been thinking." When the analyst said that she felt she had to make amends, to try to be his best patient, and to make sure that neither of them felt any anger at any time, she replied, "Drop dead! You and your wife. You can both drop dead. I'll do what I want. You just wait and see. You said you can't stop me from dying. Well, you won't stop me!" He replied, "You're frightened of me now. But I haven't changed from yesterday. I wonder what has happened since you were here yesterday." She was silent for nearly twenty minutes. She then said she had been thinking of all the things she was not going to talk about, of having masturbated after intercourse with her boyfriend, and of not caring any longer what was going to happen. She was afraid to tell the analyst that after intercourse she often had to masturbate because she could not have a climax during intercourse. This humiliated her and at the same time "it means we're back to my keeping secrets from everybody. Jim doesn't know about this, and I think he's stupid because he doesn't know." The analyst said, "I wonder what I don't know, and I wonder why I have to force you to tell me."

"I'm going to kill myself. That's what you don't know. There's no hope, I know it." On the previous day she had been with a girlfriend from the university and had thought enviously that this girl had nice breasts—nicer than her own. She had wanted to touch them. When she came home, she wanted to have intercourse with Jim immediately, but even that had not helped. After intercourse, she looked at herself and felt that she did not look nice enough. The analyst reminded her of what they had talked about in the previous session. She said she had completely forgotten that she felt she was not good enough for him, that he did not want her. "Anyway, you know about all my dirt, so you wouldn't want me. I'm surprised you still see me, after what you know." The analyst said, "You mean you are surprised that you haven't driven me away."

When she came on the following Monday, Jane told the analyst that she had been to a party over the weekend and had become drunk. Jim had not minded too much because he had too
much to drink as well. She had made a fool of herself, and she
did not care. Well, that was not true, because she really cared
very much. When she awoke the next morning, she felt that
she had humiliated herself and that Jim too must have felt humiliated because of the way she had behaved. The acting out of
part of the transference could be interpreted at this point—
that is, her humiliation was in relation to the analyst, and her
behavior at the party was her need to live out a part of the daydream she felt she could not be rid of. When he reminded her
of her earlier efforts to break down her father by presenting
herself in the nude and feeling rejected by him when he did
not respond as she had hoped he would, she replied, "You
don't care what I do, do you? If you did care, maybe you would
tell me not to get drunk."

For some time, the themes of humiliating herself, of fooling
people, and of having a secret from everybody remained the
central ones. Jane's guilt was enormous, and the combination
of this guilt with her feeling that she would "go on being abnormal" (feel attracted at times to girls, prefer masturbation to
intercourse, and be unable to have a climax during intercourse)
continued to make her feel that she must not give up "the final
weapon" (as she described it) of being able to kill herself. In the
sessions her sudden outbursts of crying and screaming, followed by very quiet speech, were part of her fantasy that the
analyst was the only person who could give her a climax and, in
that sense, enable her to become normal or, at least, to forget
"those secrets that I can't get rid of."

This primal scene material dominated Jane's analysis for
many months. Reconstruction was limited up to this point, but
there was obviously an important change in Jane's relationship
to her illness and in her feeling that she was the victim of both
her daydreams and her abnormal thoughts. She was often
frightened of falling asleep—that is, of being overwhelmed by
frightening thoughts that she could temporarily control in waking life. Although her fear of being abnormal was still certainly
present, she seemed to have less need to feel that she "must

die." Some of this improvement or this lessened vulnerability to her need to humiliate herself and then attack her body was shown in a dream she reported. This dream was in some ways similar to the one described earlier, but Jane's ability to deal with the enormous anxiety aroused by the dream was now quite different.

In this dream, Jane was being masturbated by a school friend, a girl, who suddenly withdrew her finger as Jane was being sexually aroused. From Jane's associations to the dream, we could again make the link to her feeling that she and her sister were masturbating each other and that she might prefer this to intercourse. Again we could also make the link to Jane's feeling during masturbation that she was really being held by her mother and that this was how she imagined the perfect primal scene. The difference now was that Jane seemed much more able to deal *actively* with the anxiety that had been aroused by this dream. She still referred to it as "a nightmare," but she was much less disorganized by it. She could now say that she knew she would not masturbate whenever she was alone and that now she was beginning to feel able to "feel alone without feeling also that I must die." (Jane was referring to the time earlier in her treatment when she masturbated often. She felt out of control then, and she remembered correctly that extensive masturbation was a signal that she was becoming much more seriously disturbed.)

Throughout the rest of Jane's treatment, she and the analyst both knew that she was still very vulnerable and that there was much to understand in her behavior and pathology. But, at the same time, she felt much more able to make the effort to overcome "that part of myself which is abnormal." The secrets were still there, or at least Jane felt they were. The idea of killing her body as a way of ridding herself of these secrets decreased, although, by the time her treatment terminated, these feelings had not quite disappeared. Even though she felt much more in charge of her future, she did not feel that she had rid herself completely of her persecutors.

The material reported here is a fragment of Jane's analysis. Certain parts have been chosen to highlight some aspects of her pathology and its relation to some technical problems. The analytic work was consistently directed toward the pathology and did not include those parts of Jane's behavior that represent normal developmental stresses of adolescence.

A critical point in the treatment came with the recognition of the compelling quality of some of Jane's behavior and then of the connection between this compelling quality and her central masturbation fantasy. Compelling behavior is present in the lives of many seriously disturbed adolescents, and understanding it in the transference can be critical in a number of ways. The compelling behavior can be understood as a communication to the analyst that the adolescent feels out of control and hopeless. It can be understood as the only means available to the adolescent of communicating an otherwise forbidden "memory" or wish (Freud 1914; Strachey 1934; Katan 1975). It can be used by the analyst to predict the likelihood of a serious crisis in the adolescent's life and in the treatment. But, ultimately, its understanding is essential in the treatment of adolescent psychopathology.

10
Developmental Foreclosure

Certain adolescents who, although eager to come for treatment, find it almost impossible to take an active part in reversing their existing psychopathology. We are not referring to those adolescents who have experienced a developmental breakdown at puberty and whose treatment predictably includes a range of problems and crises that may seriously jeopardize the continuation of treatment. Instead, we refer to adolescents whose pathology seems to have a different course and outcome. We have in mind those who come to treatment with a pathology that is much more defined and "complete." For them the developmental process of adolescence not only has been interfered with as the result of the breakdown at puberty but has come to a premature end, which is signified by a structured and less reversible, even irreversible, pathology.

For these adolescents, the period from puberty to adulthood is not a time for integration of the sexually mature genitals as part of the body image. Instead, their sexuality and their choice of sexual object have been ultimately determined soon after puberty with no change able to take place later in adolescence—there has been a foreclosure in the developmental process.

CLINICAL MATERIAL: David

When David, aged eighteen, came for help, he described at length his depression, his difficulty in his studies, and his uncertainty about which road to take—he was gifted in both philosophy and art. Initially, in the first interview, he referred only to his loneliness. The analyst told him that his story did not yet fit together, and he wanted to meet David a few times to try to define what it was David thought the analyst could help him with. It took a number of interviews to establish for both of them that analysis should be the treatment of choice.

All his relationships were homosexual, and he said he felt that he was now deciding to live a homosexual life. Nobody knew of this. But by now David had a large number of ongoing relationships with men—each one being sexual at some point, including anal intercourse, fellatio, being overpowered by or overpowering his partner, and every so often joining in an orgy, which meant a range of sexual experiences in one night with many men.

At the beginning of the analysis the analyst was well aware that he himself would be competing with the more magnetic and compelling gratifications David received from his relationships to other men, but the analyst felt that David's depression and his extreme anxiety about losing anyone might be allies in the treatment and in the possible undoing of the pathology. David knew from the start that the analyst did not accept his view that homosexuality was as normal as any other form of sexuality. David was clearly a highly gifted young man, but his functioning contained signs that there were transitory losses of contact with the world around him, during which time he felt enveloped by his fantasy. He would travel on buses for hours at a time, ultimately ending up at his starting point. During this time he felt cut off from the real world, hoping only that he would be "found" by a beautiful man. Or he would spend his evenings dancing at a club, acting as a "man" for part of the evening, and then would feel that he was "changing."

David's early communications in the analysis revolved around the closeness to his mother, who he felt had experienced episodes of madness during his childhood, and his father, who, although highly successful in his work, David felt was a failure in the home. His memories of his preadolescence were of a frightened, isolated child, revered by his parents, who considered him brilliant, but frightened of other children at school, who most often ignored him. He was an only child, and he remembered spending many free hours painting landscapes for his mother, who would sit by him in ecstasy. When he was six years old, he had his first sexual relationship with another boy, which consisted of mutual fellatio. Various sexual experiences continued throughout his preadolescence—mutual masturbation, fellatio, hugging, or masturbation to pictures of male athletes. Soon after puberty anal penetration of or by the partner became a regular activity. His relationships throughout adolescence were characterized by leaving or being left, disappointing the partner or being disappointed, but always with a number of men available.

In the transference, the analyst soon became the failed father who could not do anything right. He became the person who was trying to take away David's homosexuality. David wanted to feel close to him, but he felt the analyst was not permitting this. David talked at length about his art, his staying up half the night to read books on philosophy, and every so often he would tell the analyst about the man with whom he had spent the previous night. David began to taunt him with a long list of the beautiful men who loved him. But interpretations at this point were directed mainly at his disappointment and his feeling that these beautiful men still left him feeling alone and empty and that these men helped him feel that the analyst was a failure.

The analyst called attention to David's fear of coming to treatment, but he did not try to interpret this simply because he did not yet know what it might mean. He could have guessed at its meaning—fear of closeness, fear of giving in, wish for the analyst's closeness so that David could then destroy him, for example. Instead, the analyst repeatedly referred to the discrepancy between David's feeling that the world was perfect if he had a beautiful sexual partner and his private feeling that nothing was worthwhile and that he must never allow himself to feel sad. He reported a dream of a man lying on a diving board in a swimming pool, with the man and the diving board being underwater. The man looked contented but dead. This dream was the beginning of the reconstruction of the breakdown at puberty, but David terminated treatment before it could be fully understood or worked through.

The dream led to his telling the analyst of the hours he spent in his room lying on the floor, feeling unable to get up. At his work he had had a sexual relationship with another male employee, after which this person did not even bother to greet him on the street. David then went to his room, contemplated suicide, and spent about seven hours lying on the floor feeling that something in him had died. He became so frightened by this, thinking that he would jump out of the window, that he ran from the room and wandered the streets for most of the night.

His reluctance to continue the analysis had to do with his immediate fear that the analyst would force him to remember what had happened that day. He accused the analyst of taking away the men who made him happy, saying that he had never again thought of the episode at his work until the analyst forced him to have such a dream and to remember this terrible time. The excitement in the sessions—of the analyst's getting into him and making David one with him—was included in interpretations. But he did not lose sight of the fact that, for the present, this excitement was much less important than the anxiety and the meaning of the experience of feeling so desperate when David lay on the floor for hours. Nothing was any good, and his own physical beauty meant nothing if the analyst reminded him of his inability to hold on to somebody who could love him. He could then "admit" that he still resorted to lying on the floor for hours and that he often still spent half the night feeling that everything was black and hopeless.

He recalled his astonishment when he was first able to ejaculate and the accompanying feeling that his mother would be horrified if she knew. He tried for nearly a year and a half after puberty to speak in a high-pitched voice. He remembered secretly lying on the floor during this time in his room, crying and wanting his mother to tell him that she would go on loving him for his art. The longing for the father had never been conscious, and transference interpretations did not make this longing have any emotional significance for him.

David talked of his past, but his memories were very restricted, and he was clearly frightened about coming into touch with a past that he felt he had idealized and then lost. The focus at that point was on the immediate past and on the emotional experiences, which were still alive but frightening. Transference interpretations were directed primarily at the different ways he experienced the analyst in relation to his male sexual partners, at David's longing for him as a sexual partner, and at David's wish both to be loved by him and to destroy his potency. David's hatred of his mother and his accusations toward her, which occurred often in dreams, were sometimes included in interpretations, but the analyst concentrated mainly on his fear of the women at his work and his discomfort and anxiety in being treated as a potent man.

The first details of the content of his central masturbation fantasy came via the repetition of fellatio experiences with men, the efforts to force the analyst to attack and hit him, and the satisfaction he described he would get from men after anal penetration and hugging one another. Toward the latter part of treatment the idea of oneness with the object when he was penetrated anally became an important theme. But by the time treatment was terminated, no significant understanding of the content of this fantasy had been reached.

Just after a year of treatment, David met a man slightly older than himself whom he considered to be the perfect male. When things were going well with this man, treatment had no place in his life. He began to come late, then began to stay away. If he was disappointed because this man had become angry with him or had threatened to leave, David demanded that the analyst try to do something to make sure that he would not be left. Nothing else mattered now. He stayed away from his work, sat in his room telephoning the man hour after hour and begging for forgiveness. When this man gave up David for another man, he felt that there was little purpose in being alive and contemplated killing himself. But, after a few weeks, he decided to give up his job and sought work in another city. When he was offered a position away from London, he then became worried about losing the analyst and being alone. The analyst discussed with David the various possible consequences if he decided to terminate treatment, but he nevertheless decided to stop. Before ending, he told the analyst that, while in this other city seeking employment, he had met a man who he believed could give him what he now wanted. He seemed aware that his future relationships would be homosexual and that he would be vulnerable to severe depression. But he felt that the analyst could not protect him from the hurt and humiliation of being left for another man. Nor did he feel that he had any interest in women. "I know they are there, but I don't even notice."

Although he seemed anxious about ending treatment, the gratification David felt as the result of the fantasied triumph over the analyst made his leaving a necessity.

In David's case, all his sexual experiences during childhood and adolescence were with other males. Before adolescence, he had already had relationships with boys with whom he could live out his fantasy of being both male and female. During latency and throughout adolescence his fantasies were not contained in masturbation through trial action but were lived out with other males in fellatio, by being penetrated and by penetrating them anally. During these sexual experiences he felt united with them, and the sought-after perfection was found. After puberty these sexual experiences always included ejaculation, which meant that his central masturbation fantasy was being lived out in these experiences and that *developmentally his main means of gratification had become established prematurely* (A. Freud 1965; Glover 1933; Gillespie 1964), with the result that the period of adolescence could not make any further contribution to the outcome of his sexual organization.

Many adolescents come to treatment with characteristics that seem similar to David's, but their treatment may progress differently, and their pathology may be reversible through treatment. One critical difference between these adolescents and David is that their object choices are determined more by anxiety and a regression to a preincestuous object relationship; whereas for David the choice of sexual object and the means of sexual gratification were determined by the integration of distorted genitals, which then resulted in a distorted body image and confirmed his earlier break with reality. For David, puberty and the period of adolescence fixed the earlier distortion of reality; the sexual experiences and the sexual body—the fellatio, the anal penetration—made it possible for the earlier pregenital gratifications to become genital and incestuous and therefore perverse (Chasseguet-Smirgel 1981; Deutsch 1932; Ferenczi 1913). For David, unlike those adolescents whose behavior is determined more by anxiety and regression, the period of adolescence acted as a time of confirmation of his distortion of or break with reality. In such cases, we would say that there has been a *foreclosure* of the developmental process, with the implication that pathology has been fixed well before the end of adolescence and is much less likely to be reversible.

When David was encouraged to decide on analytic treatment, the analyst was aware that the treatment could not compete with the gratification that existed away from treatment. David never really doubted his choice of homosexuality. But the analyst felt that David's severe depression might be the ally in the treatment. The mistake lay in the analyst's belief that the experience in the transference and the working through of the breakdown at puberty could offer David a different hope and could help him give up the need to destroy the oedipal objects by destroying his own sexual body. The analyst did not foresee David's inability to experience the frustration of the transference relationship, with the implied promise of more satisfactory gratification and object relationships in the future. By "more satisfactory" we refer to removing the perpetual threat of abandonment and despair and also to the ability to maintain a closer link with the external world and to give up the distortions that at one time were the only means available to maintain a sense of narcissistic equilibrium. Instead, David was compelled to repeat the manic triumph over the oedipal father and to perpetuate the hatred of his mother (Greenson 1968). The destruction of his genital sexuality maintained a relationship to his idealized body but at the same time interfered with the possibility that the breakdown at puberty could be reexperienced and worked through in the analysis. The analyst represented the person who would bring him into touch with the frightening depression and with the meaning of his hatred. David decided to leave treatment when he became aware that he was beginning to allow the analyst to create doubt about his present sexual organization.

The dynamic difference in adolescent psychopathology between "perverse" and "regressive" has important bearing on the likelihood of the pathology being reversed through treatment. By "perverse" we imply a fixed pathology; by "regressive" we assume the continuation of the developmental process where the sexual body image and the ultimate male-female differentiation become fixed only by the end of adolescence. Such dynamic differences may also apply to other manifestations of severe developmental breakdown, such as behavior which descriptively includes delusions, melancholic-type responses, or paranoid projections resulting in ideas of reference. Such manifestations of psychopathology must be assessed with great caution because of the easy possibility of viewing them as signs of the presence of psychosis. In adolescence, this need not be so, and such a diagnosis would be a grave error. Instead, we can apply the criteria suggested here of "fixed" pathology versus pathology that still allows for the continuation of the developmental process.

11
Countertransference and the Adolescent's Sexual Development

An important part of the psychoanalyst's work in assessment or treatment is the need to decide whether certain forms of sexual activity or behavior are signs of abnormality. In work with the adolescent, such a judgment becomes critical because it is a judgment about the person's sense of reality, his relation to himself as a sexual and social being, as well as his future psychological state.

In this chapter, we discuss the issues that must be part of the undertaking of assessment or treatment and that affect day-to-day work with the adolescent. These are (1) whether certain forms of sexual activity and behavior during adolescence invariably represent a disruption in psychological development; (2) whether such disruption, if it exists, justifies regarding such activity and behavior as "abnormal"; and (3) whether the psychoanalyst should or should not make a judgment about this activity and behavior.

Although the implications of the adolescent's present sexual activity may be difficult to assess, it is nevertheless crucial to hold a view about the likely effect of various sexual activities and relationships on the person's sexual orientation. We have in mind homosexuality, fetishism, transvestitism, and other perverse sexual activities in adolescence.

Developmental breakdown in adolescence can manifest itself in a range of ways, and at times it may not be obvious. But certain forms of sexual activity always signify that a developmental breakdown has taken place. The way we define our function in

work with the adolescent and the judgments we make about
the normality or abnormality of certain forms of sexual activity
or behavior are linked directly to the views we have about the
developmental function of adolescence, the meaning of developmental breakdown, and the prospects for future mental
health or psychopathology. These views are elaborated in earlier chapters.[1]

Here we include another factor that is relevant to the issue of
judging whether certain forms of sexual activity or behavior
are normal or abnormal. An important task of development
during adolescence is *the restoration of the oedipal parents*—that
is, the ability by the end of adolescence to begin to forgive the
internalized parents for not having protected the original
childhood state of narcissistic perfection (Loewald 1979).
Viewed in terms of the oedipal relationship to one's adolescence, this means that by the end of adolescence there should
be the ability unconsciously to test the oedipal disappointments
and the jealousy and envy of *both* parents in ways that remove
the blaming of the oedipal parents for the earlier failures. Expressed in terms of genitality, it means that by the end of adolescence there is the internal freedom to acknowledge unconsciously that the original oedipal wish and demand contained
an unfulfillable fantasy of the perpetuation of perfection and
of ultimately acquiring the oedipal parent. Instead, during adolescence and especially by the end of adolescence, the person
can, in normal development, be free to use oedipal identifications to enable him to include the functioning genitals in the
body image (Blos 1977; Freud 1924; Greenacre 1969). The adolescent is then able to feel that genitality is his right, given to
him by the oedipal parents, and this right removes any need or
wish to destroy that genitality. This is what is meant by "ownership of the body," a process that is normally completed by the
end of adolescence.[2]

But certain forms of sexual activity and behavior represent at
the least a breakdown in the developmental process of adoles-

1. See chapters 1, 2, and 6.
2. See chapter 3.

cence and carry unconsciously a statement about the adolescent's relationship to his own sexual body, which is now identified with that of the oedipal parent. Those who manifest this behavior have not been able to use adolescence as a time when they can begin to make amends in their relationship with the oedipal parents—that is, they have not been able, through their genitality, to identify with the parents' sexuality. Instead, they use their bodies to live out the fantasy of the destruction of the oedipal mother—the one who remains blamed for having robbed the child, who is now an adolescent, of the perfect union and the original narcissistic perfection. In adolescence, these people are compelled to destroy their own genitality and to continue to portray the destruction of their physically mature genitals. This holds true for those who, by the end of adolescence, no longer have any choice but to accept certain kinds of sexual activity and relationships as the main expression of their sexuality, as is the case in homosexuality, fetishism, transvestitism, and perversions (Limentani 1977; Stoller 1969).

The additional danger for these adolescents is that the "giving in" also means that the fantasies produced during adolescence, instead of being used actively in the attempt to alter the central masturbation fantasy, become integrated into the adolescent's pathological sexual organization and strengthen the quality and the extent of the developmental breakdown. The unconscious hatred and blaming of the oedipal parent may be the outcome in the lives of many adolescents, whether or not their sexual activity and relationships include people of the opposite sex. For those who have the internal ability to establish heterosexual relationships and who can rely on physical genitality as the main means of sexual gratification, however, there may still be the possibility of doubting their previous internal solutions and of reversing the damage of the developmental breakdown.

The choice of sexual object during adolescence, and especially by the end of adolescence, represents the manner in which genital sexuality has or has not been integrated into the final sexual organization. In other words, one's relation to the oedipal objects, to one's own sexual body, and to the external world also represent one's relation to reality. It is only with the need ultimately to give up the original oedipal wishes that reality testing may finally be established. This oedipal solution in relation to reality should again be questioned in adolescence and re-resolved by the end of adolescence. Those adolescents who have rejected or denied their genitality and who unconsciously have to continue to use their sexual bodies and the sexual object to confirm their self-hatred and the hatred of the oedipal parent, however, do not question their original relation to reality during adolescence. Their present relation to reality, then, must be seriously interfered with (Chasseguet-Smirgel 1981). Their self-hatred and their need to destroy their genitality strengthen the distortions and ultimately force them to give in forever. Unless they are able *during adolescence* to question their original solutions and to be helped to add meaning to their oedipal hatred and rejection of the identification with the oedipal parent of the same sex, these adolescents will have lost their chance forever to question and reverse the direction of their lives.

The rejection during adolescence of one's body as being either masculine or feminine means that the person has irreversibly rejected the oedipal identification with the parent of the same sex. It means that the person's relationship to his or her own body, if the object choice is homosexual or one in which the genitals are not the primary vehicle for sexual gratification and for the love of the sexual object, also contains the hopelessness with which he or she has lived since childhood. In such relationships, the function of procreation is denied or seems irrelevant. But the possibility of choice of procreation during adolescence is central to a person's efforts to establish sexual identity. The ability to choose to be a father or a mother is a necessary part of a person's relationship to himself as a male or herself as a female and is fundamental in ultimately establishing the relation to his or her past. Those relationships that, through their sexual activity, exclude the possibility of procreation strengthen the distortion of the sexual body image and must at the same time strengthen the self-hatred and hatred of the oedipal object. Such relationships break a link with the past. In terms of the person's present life, they may also strengthen the feeling that his past has nothing to do with him, that he is simply the product of parents who hated him and who withheld the right to genital sexuality (Lampl-de Groot 1962; Harley 1961).

COUNTERTRANSFERENCE

When the psychoanalyst undertakes to try to help the adolescent, he implicitly agrees that the adolescent will be offered the chance to examine those areas of his present and past life that have brought about the existing problems and are now part of the adolescent's internal life. He also undertakes to help the adolescent get more in touch with those factors or experiences in his life that have determined the choice he has made or wishes to make about his present and future life.

The adolescent may agree with the analyst's undertaking, or he may feel that he has the right to make any choice he likes without any need for the analyst to question that choice. But this view cannot be accepted by the analyst from the start, because there is an important difference between the person's conscious intent or choice and the unconscious factors that determine "choice." The great difficulty the adolescent has in acknowledging and accepting the presence of factors in his life other than the conscious ones, together with the extreme power of pathology, may force the vulnerable or potentially ill adolescent to reject any definition or understanding of his behavior other than that which is conscious. He may also have to deny the authority of the past, and he may feel that any choice other than the one he has made consciously is a submission to the past—that is, a submission to the oedipal parent who he feels was responsible initially for his present mental state.

The analyst may make the error of confusing his moral and ethical views about people's rights and his responsibility when choosing to work with people whose future psychological lives are still being determined and finalized. If we accept that certain forms of sexual activity or behavior during adolescence are, at the least, a sign of developmental breakdown, then our primary responsibility is to try to keep open the potential of choice that may still exist for this adolescent. If we apply our views about people's rights to our function in assessment and treatment of the adolescent, we take the risk of confirming the adolescent's unconscious belief that there is no hope, that he is worthless, and that the oedipal parent has given up any wish for him to be a sexual being and the owner of his sexual body. The adolescent who seeks help may wish for this kind of confirmation, but at the same time he may also wish for the analyst to doubt the choices he has made until now and to offer the possibility of a different solution. As the result of treatment, the adolescent may feel that he can now choose actively to live his social and psychological life in one way or another. He may, in fact, decide to continue to live a life that is, for example, homosexual in terms of his choice of sexual partner. Or he may understand that the only relationships he can value, and perhaps the only ones he can have in the first place, exclude genital sexuality. This may be an outcome of treatment, but it is based on his readiness to question and to doubt his earlier solutions.

Developmental breakdown in adolescence, as expressed by the choice of "sexual abnormality," means that the adolescent has given up hope of ever restoring the relationship to the oedipal parent. But by choosing "sexual abnormality" and giving up the hope of restoring the relationship to the oedipal parent, he also defies his conscience and thereby breaks the relationship to his own past—that is, he gives up feeling that his past and his present life are in any way his responsibility. But if the adolescent has agreed to undertake treatment, he has chosen to give the psychoanalyst the right to question his earlier solutions. In this sense, the psychoanalyst's "neutrality" is therefore untenable; inasmuch as it is contrary to the undertaking of the analyst, it is also contrary to the unconscious expectation and hope of the adolescent. Neutrality is, in this context, equivalent to confirmation of the adolescent's hopelessness. It may also be experienced by the adolescent as yet another confirmation that "sexual abnormality" is the only right he has.

But the ability *not* to be neutral, especially in the face of many present-day views that consider sexual behavior such as homosexuality to be normal and a person's right, means that the psychoanalyst needs to be aware of the meaning of his own adolescence in relation to his present life. It may mean giving up many of the idealizations of the past that we live with. It may also force us to consider the extent of our own envy of the adolescent's sexuality, and it may necessitate the risk of losing some of the narcissistic gains that so many ill adolescents want to or have to offer us, especially if their pathological solutions are not questioned or, perhaps more seriously, are felt by them to be idealized or overvalued.

CLINICAL IMPLICATIONS

A number of clinical implications follow from what we have said. We will discuss only those related specifically to the issues that we defined at the beginning of the chapter—that is, to the psychoanalyst's attitude to the adolescent who seeks help and whose developmental breakdown has manifested itself by "sexual abnormality."

When we see such an adolescent for assessment or for possible treatment, we explain to him our view about sexual abnormality. We explain in detail (and if necessary we will see the adolescent a number of times for this) why we consider his present choice as a sign of the presence of serious trouble. We add that we will try to help him understand its meaning for him and how it may have come about. The adolescent knows, at the same time, that it is not our wish or intention to try remorselessly to take away his choice but that treatment does mean questioning the choice, understanding its meaning, and possibly changing.

After these terms are clear, if the adolescent insists that his sexual life and object choices must at no time be discussed or questioned but that we must concentrate on some other area of his problems, we choose not to accept him for treatment. We are aware of the view held by some colleagues that treatment might ultimately lead to this examination and understanding and that there is no need at the start of treatment to take such a firm view. Our experience has shown that many adolescents who come for treatment expect to be either fooled or forced to submit. They then may continue in treatment because of the transference relationship that has been established but without any lasting therapeutic work going on. Those adolescents whose sexual lives include sexual abnormality very often feel that they have been fooled or cheated in the past and are convinced that the oedipal object, represented now by the psychoanalyst, wants them to remain as they are. Although this view can be understood during treatment, it is important from the start to separate oneself from this expectation and to enable the adolescent to choose to accept treatment or not.

But when we say that the adolescent can choose treatment or not, we do not simply allow him to decide totally on his own. We discuss with him our views about his present life and tell him why there is reason to be worried and why he should consider having treatment. We also make it clear *from the start* that we do make judgments that have to do with his present and future life. Adolescents may find it extremely difficult to separate our judgment about normality or abnormality from the judgment of right or wrong, good or bad. Within the transference, however, the meaning of right or wrong, good or bad, becomes a central factor and is something that has existed in the adolescent's life for years past, especially from puberty onward. To imply that we do not judge is equivalent to avoiding the issue of normality or abnormality, breakdown or not. Beyond this, however, the adolescent is certainly aware that we are making a judgment, and for us not to acknowledge this from the start of treatment represents for him both collusion and an opting out by us.

From the start of treatment, we acknowledge the extent of the adolescent's suffering, even though he himself may insist that his life is proceeding well. Often, the adolescent will feel that to admit to any suffering is to risk losing the only people or things who offer any pleasure or who make him feel worthwhile. This anxiety has to be acknowledged from the start, but at the same time it is also critical to acknowledge the extent of his aloneness and inner emptiness. The adolescent is aware from the outset that we view his present life and his choices as signs of the presence of severe trouble within himself, and he knows that it is not possible for us to be neutral.

IV
ASSESSMENT

12
Assessment of Psychopathology in Adolescence

The application of the developmental model of adolescence to the assessment of psychopathology means that we should aim:

1. to establish whether a developmental breakdown has occurred;
2. to establish the extent of the present vulnerability—that is, how far the defensive maneuvers the adolescent feels forced to employ (to deal with the anxiety aroused as the result of the developmental breakdown) are successful in enabling him to continue to feel in control of his functioning;
3. to attempt to predict the extent of the vulnerability the adolescent may be left with by the end of adolescence, once the final sexual organization has become established.

We have often seen adolescents in whose cases we felt that decisions had been made mistakenly about pathology, treatment, or management because these decisions were not based on the meaning of the immediate problem and its significance for the future emotional development of the adolescent. When an adolescent complains of being depressed and feeling that life is not worth living, on what basis should we see this as a sign of serious pathology? If it is normal to feel depressed at times during adolescence, how depressed must an adolescent be before we view it as a sign of illness? Or, if an adolescent displays his disturbance more overtly by symptomatic behavior or even by an inability to function, how can we go beyond simply using existing psychiatric categories to assess what we are seeing? Decisions about any form of intervention must take into account the damage that has occurred and continues to occur in the developmental process and the vulnerability to mental disturbance or illness in adulthood this must leave with the adolescent. Disturbances during adolescence are frequently handled on a symptomatic basis by prescribing drugs or by offering help in dealing with the current external conflicts; if the disturbed behavior affects society at large, there may be greater emphasis on control of the adolescent. The adolescent may be aware that this is no answer to his problems, but at the same time he may feel forced to accept it as the only help available to him. The implicit assumption is that if the adolescent can be helped over his current emotional crisis, or at times into accepting himself as an ill person, this is all the help that may be needed or should be given.

But the task of making a diagnostic decision is much more complex because it must include an assessment of the extent to which normal progressive development has already been interfered with, to be used then as a basis for the decision about the focus and intensity of therapeutic efforts. Adolescence is a time when the person may be especially vulnerable to emotional disturbance, and diagnostically it is a time when we may be able to observe the early signs of potentially serious future trouble. This provides us with a unique opportunity to intervene in a way that may prevent finding a pathologically based solution to the developmental tasks of the adolescent period. However difficult the task may be, it is one that does not allow room for error or failure because wrong assessment may affect the whole future of the adolescent.

ASSESSMENT AND BREAKDOWN

In earlier chapters we described the clinical observations that led us to conceptualize our thinking that serious emotional disorders during adolescence result from a breakdown in the developmental process following the impact of puberty on the equilibrium within the mental structures. We have described how this developmental breakdown represents the adolescent's inability to allow his body image to change so that it will include the sexually mature genitals and to permit this image of himself to become differentiated into male or female. Instead, the psychopathology represents the defensive measures that the adolescent has available to avoid or prevent such changes from taking place.

In assessment, then, we are primarily trying to decide whether there is evidence that a breakdown occurred at puberty and, if so, how severe the present interference is in the developmental process.

I. CATEGORIES OF ASSESSMENT

Three main categories of assessment can be applied. These categories refer to the extent of disruption in development, the nature of the distortion of the adolescent's relation to himself as a sexually mature person, and the extent to which the adolescent's link with external reality is impaired. They are:

A. development that is dominated by *defensive functioning*;
B. *deadlock* in development that precipitates an acute crisis in functioning;
C. *foreclosure* in development, where there is a premature end to the developmental process.

Defensive functioning can be divided into (1) that which allows some progressive development to take place—where it appears as if only one specific area of the adolescent's life is affected, and (2) that which appears to dominate the whole of the adolescent's functioning—his capacity to work and make new relationships, for example. In the latter case the danger is that a total breakdown in functioning may take place in the near future as the adolescent becomes progressively unable to defend against the anxiety he is attempting to deal with. The nature of the defensive process tells us the specific area being defended against. How far the defensive process is dominating all other functioning is conveyed by the extent to which the actual body of the adolescent is involved in the defensive process.

In the younger adolescent, when the primary task is of effecting a change in the body image itself into one that can include the potent genitals, defensive functioning will always be directly linked to anxiety about the body. Later, however, we should see the compromises that the adolescent begins to make when he starts testing out his sexual body in new relationships and work choices. But if the defensive process is still primarily related to integration of the sexual body image, it must now create an interference that will dominate and interfere with the total functioning of the adolescent. In order to assess the seriousness of this interference, we must examine the extent to which the adolescent is compelled to attack his own body or show his rejection of it by neglect or indifference and compare this to the extent to which there are also signs that the adolescent is able to feel that his sexual body contains potential for pleasurable experiences on libidinal and narcissistic levels.

Deadlock may be defined as the point at which the defensive process that was initially able to contain anxiety fails to do so. There is no possibility for development to proceed, nor is there the alternative of regressive functioning because this, too, is experienced as a source of anxiety. For example, the eighteen-year-old who experiences the breakup of his first sexual relationship as confirmation that his male sexual body is unacceptable—the original breakdown at puberty is now contained in the rejection of his sexual body—can no longer see himself as a prepubertal child who may find reassurance from his oedipal objects. In such a situation of deadlock there is a serious risk that the adolescent will be precipitated into an acute psychotic episode—that is, a temporary break with reality that is manic or depressive and suicidal.

The anxiety the adolescent has about his sexual body may appear to be totally contained by a preoccupation with a specific aspect of his body, such as a fixed idea of needing to change some part of the body. This is a sign that the adolescent has been unable to contain the anxiety about his body; the threat of becoming overwhelmed has effected a split in his sexual body image so that only a part of it has to be rejected. In this way the adolescent can avoid a situation of complete deadlock despite the overwhelming anxiety that is being defended against.

Foreclosure means that the developmental process has ended prematurely, with the integration of a distorted body image and the ability to ward off or ignore any experiences that may create doubt in the solution found. There is an absence of anxiety. The main means of sexual gratification has been established without the adolescent's having been able to allow for any change of earlier solutions to conflict.[1]

We include in this category those people whose sexual gratification, although of an abnormal kind, enables them to establish a sexual relationship (e.g., perverse, homosexual). We also include adolescents whose lives are dominated by some form of addiction and for whom relationships are secondary to the gratification obtained from the addiction.

II. CRITERIA FOR ASSESSMENT

The criteria to which we give priority in our assessment of psychopathology are linked to our definition of the developmental function of adolescence—that is, the establishment of the final sexual organization. The extent of developmental interference that exists can be used as a reliable guide in establishing whether a developmental breakdown has occurred. In particular, we want to establish the extent to which the adolescent appears to be rejecting his sexual body and the means he uses to maintain this rejection. This can enable us to establish the direction of development of his sexual organization and can convey whether development is still taking place or has ended prematurely. Such an assessment can also clarify the extent to which the adolescent's link with reality has been damaged. We examine the following areas:

A. *Direction of Libido*: The extent to which the adolescent appears to be dependent on autoerotic gratification, avoidance of gratification, or dependent on objects for gratification;

B. *Object Relationships*: Whether, and to what extent, the adolescent is able to distinguish between his projected image

1. See chapter 10.

of himself and the external reality of the people he is relating to (including the oedipal objects);

C. *Relation to Oedipal Objects*: The extent to which the adolescent still feels dependent on the oedipal objects, as well as
the anxiety related to identification with unacceptable aspects of them;

D. *Means of Gratification*: What are the indications that genital dominance over other forms of gratification is being
achieved? Do the present means of nongenital gratification succeed in avoiding anxiety about failure to reach
genitality?;

E. *Male-Female Identifications*: What are the signs that the adolescent is able to identify with the parent of the same sex
without feeling overwhelmed by anxiety?;

F. *Relation to Anxiety*: To what extent can the adolescent allow
himself to be conscious of anxiety—is the tendency toward
denial, manic states, inhibition, or suppression?;

G. *Relation to Other Emotions*: Is the adolescent able to relate to
himself as someone who experiences emotions such as depression, anger, or excitement?;

H. *Relation to External Reality*: To what extent is the adolescent
able to relate to external events, or does he remain isolated
within his inner world and emotional state?;

I. *Compelling Actions and Behavior*: How far are the actions or
behavior under the dominance of an unconscious need of a
repetitive and compelling nature? How far can these be
modified through the influence of external reality, such as
danger to life, to self-esteem, to future success, to being in
charge of one's own actions as compared with putting oneself under the control of authority (as in delinquent behavior)?;

J. *Self-Observation*: To what extent is the adolescent able to observe himself independently of the picture of himself he at-
tributes to others?

We do not wish to detract from the importance of noting
and assessing the adolescent's overall functioning—social relationships; attitude to the future; attitude to anxiety; attitude to

school or work; sublimations; frustration tolerance—but this would not enable us to establish the presence and extent of the developmental breakdown that has taken place. Instead, a picture of the adolescent's overall functioning would help us establish with greater certainty the extent to which there is either an active seeking for progressive development or a passive wish to give in to the existing disorder. Although this, too, represents the adolescent's relationship to his own sexual body and to his adult sexuality, our assessment, if based on his overall functioning (rather than on specific areas that we have listed here), would not be exact enough and much less reliable when applied to prediction.

III. THE DEFENSIVE PROCESS

The areas of functioning just described enable us to get an overall picture of the defensive process and the defense mechanisms employed. By understanding the meaning of the events following puberty in the life of the adolescent in terms of such a detailed examination, we can construct a view of the point to which the adolescent was able to proceed in his development without obvious interference—for instance, the establishment of his first heterosexual relationship or a certain level of achievement at school—and how the defensive process that we can now observe is related to this point in his development. Has the breakdown in the relationship resulted in an attack on his sexual body or in a withdrawal from objects into a narcissistic state? Has it led to a renewed dependence on the oedipal objects, but one that now contains the projection of the adolescent's hatred of himself for this dependence? Has the depression resulted in a withdrawal from objects to narcissistic preoccupation or autoerotic activity?

As well as establishing the point at which the breakdown became manifest in the adolescent's life, the actual details of the defensive process will enable an assessment to be made of the extent of the adolescent's present vulnerability. Does the defensive process that is initiated now become a source of anxiety rather than contain it (for example, those adolescents who, when needing to become dependent again on the oedipal objects as the result of a crisis, feel helpless in the face of their incestuous wishes or their projections on to the oedipal object)?

In assessment we are concerned with those defensive processes that indicate that there is some failure in integrating the body image and that the defensive process itself is now dominating the adolescent's functioning in such a way that we may conclude that a breakdown in development has taken place. In order to distinguish between defensive processes that enable development to proceed and those that constitute a breakdown in development, we have to establish how directly the process involves the adolescent's body and whether there is the ability to use the sexual body in a pleasurable way, both libidinally and narcissistically. Or, what are the indications that, in experiences which directly involve his sexual body, the adolescent is compelled to attack or reject his body because he can experience it only as a source of guilt or shame?

Similarly, the defense mechanisms that are of special significance are those the adolescent appears to depend on but that at the same time constitute an interference in progressive development. Dependence on defense mechanisms that impair the ability to perceive external reality (such as projection, splitting, or denial of affect) and evidence of the adolescent's inability to integrate the reality of his own sexual body and its new demands must eventually lead to a distortion of the body image to accommodate itself to the maintenance of these defenses. We need, therefore, to know how far the adolescent is able to relate to people and to the external world without the use of mechanisms (such as projection) which maintain a distorted perception and which distort his relationships. This information can enable us to define the extent to which the developmental breakdown, if it is present, is already creating a push toward psychotic functioning or a total break with reality. For example, if we see an eighteen-year-old girl who believes her mother is the source of her problems and describes her as totally irrational and helpless, we have to know how far the adolescent depends on a distorted view of her mother's "madness" to avoid any anxiety she may have about herself and whether this dependence is such that she cannot doubt her view of her mother.

The extent to which the adolescent feels forced to rely on a distorted perception of objects as a basis for all his emotions tells us about his need to believe that his sexual feelings and fantasies are the result of demands from outside. His internal reality is felt to be safe, but a break with external reality may be imminent. In assessment we are not concerned with a diagnosis of "paranoia." We want to assess how far his persecutory experiences reflect his experience of his own sexual body and whether this is now forcing him to distort his relationship to the external world. Such a distortion indicates the beginning of integration of a distorted body image and a consequent inability by the end of adolescence for a final sexual organization that allows for normal heterosexual relationships. It is from this point of view that we assess the information we obtain regarding the adolescent's relationships. Is there already a tendency toward isolation rather than the wish to seek out new sexual objects? What is the significance of the actual choice of objects? Are they chosen on the basis of defensive needs or narcissistic ones? Is the dependence on the object a source of anxiety because it is used defensively? Is the basic dependence on the oedipal object unchanged? The answers to such questions should help us in our assessment of developmental breakdown and its severity.

IV. IMPLICATIONS FOR ASSESSMENT OF SPECIFIC FORMS OF SYMPTOMATOLOGY

Certain disorders or forms of behavior occurring during adolescence can be regarded as being characteristic of the symptomatology of adolescence. Although we cannot make a comprehensive list, we include these:

A. Compulsive eating
B. Compulsive fasting
C. Sudden academic or work failure
D. Promiscuity

E. Suicide attempts
F. Self-injury
G. Perverse sexual behavior
H. Severe depression
 I. Severe phobias
 J. Compulsive masturbation
K. Absence of masturbation; inability to ejaculate
L. Drug taking and addiction (including alcoholism)
M. Bedwetting
N. Delinquency
O. Psychosomatic disorders

For purposes of assessment, these symptoms have to be evaluated similarly to those described in section III (The Defensive Process). We should concern ourselves with evaluating how far the symptom itself is a sign of a developmental breakdown having taken place and how far the actual symptomatology is now affecting the potential for further development to take place.

To do this, we would use the following questions as a guide for evaluating the seriousness of the interference with the developmental process:

1. Is the symptom related to the control or the actual rejection of the sexual body (compulsive eating or fasting or a suicide attempt, for example)?
2. Will the symptom result in failure to make object relationships (such as phobias or bedwetting)?
3. Will the symptom result in an image of the body or of oneself as damaged or unacceptable (psychosomatic disorders such as asthma or acne, or affective disorders such as depression)?

V. ADDITIONAL ISSUES OF ASSESSMENT

Other issues that are fundamental to the problem of assessment need to be considered because they directly affect our understanding of the meaning of certain clinical data:

A. When does adolescence end?
B. How do the age and sex of the adolescent affect assessment?

C. What part, if any, do we attribute to potentially traumatic real events that occur during adolescence?
D. How do we distinguish the severity of the present interference and the diagnostic implications (psychotic functioning or development toward psychosis, for example)?

When does adolescence end? When we refer to the end of adolescence, we have in mind one specific outcome that signifies the end of the developmental process, and that is *the establishment of the main means of sexual gratification*. We make a number of assumptions about the relationship between the developmental function of adolescence, the ending of adolescence, and the establishment of the main means of sexual gratification. Puberty establishes the primacy of the genital zone, and this is normally the time when the gratifications attached to infantile sexuality (and to forepleasure) begin to be kept under much stricter repression, with genital sexual gratification acting as the main source of gratification. Even though his development may be proceeding normally, the adolescent is on guard against any signs of sexual abnormality—an anxiety which is felt to be new, inasmuch as prepubertal anxiety is not related to sexual abnormality, whereas anxiety following puberty must be.

The end of adolescence is signified by the establishment of a final sexual organization or, defined in terms of relationship to the body, by the integration of the physically mature genitals as part of the body image. Male or female differentiation, although having its precursors in the phallic-oedipal period as part of the oedipal resolution, seems to become established *ultimately* and *irreversibly* only during adolescence as part of the integration of the physically mature genitals into the image of the body.

The seeking and finding of a sexual object during adolescence reaches back to the beginnings of sexual satisfaction and may be determined as part of the resolution of the oedipal conflict. But it is only during adolescence—that is, following physical sexual maturity—that the seeking and finding of a sexual object becomes a primary vehicle in the establishment of the final sexual organization. It seems that it is only by the end of adolescence that the main means of sexual gratification and the choice of sexual object become irreversibly interdependent.

When we refer to the establishment of the main means of sexual gratification, we have in mind the interrelation between the psychic and the physical—not physical sexual gratification in an isolated sense. Instead, we view physical sexual gratification as an integral part of a total psychophysical process, which includes the relationship to the object, the living out of primary fantasy content, the ability unconsciously to identify with the oedipal parent of the same sex without having to experience this as the killing of the parent, and the ability to obtain secondary narcissistic reinforcement through the object. In this sense, puberty (the presence of physically mature genitals) is experienced developmentally as a demand to integrate these genitals as part of one's narcissistic and object-related organization. Preoedipal gratifications can be allowed so long as these do not override oedipal and genital wishes. The use of the penis or the vagina, with accompanying orgasm, enables the central masturbation fantasy to be gratified while at the same time strengthening the impetus for the libido to remain object-directed.

Our experience, at least with severely disturbed adolescents, leads us to conclude that the end of adolescence takes place by age twenty-one, by which time, at the latest, a defined and predictable way of dealing with regressive manifestations and anxiety has been established. The choice of an object is by now set along a specific and definite path, which represents the means chosen unconsciously by the adolescent to maintain a level of gratification, to leave behind the oedipal strictures, and at the same time to maintain and ensure a certain level of object relatedness.

But in our work with seriously disturbed adolescents, we observed that in some cases there may also be a much earlier so-called end of adolescence—that is, a foreclosure of the developmental process brought about by the presence of psychopathology. In foreclosure, the main means of sexual gratification and the direction of the choice of object have been decided by long-standing pathological development; puberty and the period of adolescence are experienced mainly as the addition of physical genitality to the pathological organization. In these instances, either the lack of conflict, the extent of sexual gratification, or the passive submission to the conflict is enough to nullify any wish for or hope of change. For some of these adolescents, development has stopped prematurely. Foreclosure means, for them, premature integration or a premature answer to developmental conflict. Their final sexual organization and psychopathology are established at the time of the foreclosure of the developmental process.

The question of the end of adolescence is important clinically because it means that by the age of eighteen or nineteen a sense of urgency has to be added to decisions regarding therapeutic intervention. A nineteen-year-old girl, for instance, who feels that she cannot go out with friends of her own age but still feels dependent on her parents to include her in their activities is not simply "late" in her move toward independent functioning. Instead, we are seeing a sign of severe interference in development, and we can assume that without intervention some serious compromises will have been found by the age of twenty-one or twenty-two.

At nineteen, however, we can still hope to understand the nature of the ongoing interference with a view to undoing its pathological power. Once an adolescent becomes involved in the therapeutic process, time is on his side—it seems as if the therapeutic process itself, if successful, can temporarily enable the conflicts of adolescence to remain fluid.

How do the age and sex of the adolescent affect assessment? Normally, the young adolescent's primary need is to find means of reinvesting his new body image with narcissistic libido—that is, to find ways of being able to accept, rather than feel forced to reject, his new sexual body. During this period the relationships made by the adolescent will be primarily on a narcissistic basis. From the point of view of assessment, then, excessive dependence on relationships to peers should be examined to determine whether they are part of a defensive process that interferes with the normal function of masturbation or whether they are the only means available to defend against continued dependence on the oedipal objects for gratification. Isolation from peers during this period has to be viewed as a sign of failure in the adolescent's ability to experience his sexual body and its needs as acceptable.

During the later period of adolescence, after the age of sixteen or seventeen, the adolescent normally begins to seek out sexual objects whose function is to enable male-female differentiation to become integrated—objects that enable the oedipal identifications to become changed and accepted to include genitality. It is in this period that the developmental breakdown, which took place at puberty, may become obvious—he may have no ability to change the quality of his relationships, or the early tendency to avoid them may become reinforced into active isolation. We now might see how the original breakdown at puberty results in a defensive process that is distorting the external world and forcing the adolescent to withdraw from it. For such adolescents we have to assess the extent to which this already implies the beginning of a move to psychotic functioning.

If there is a marked dependence on obtaining gratification from autoerotic practices that include the distorted body image (as in anal masturbation, transvestite or fetishistic practices), the danger exists that the final sexual organization must include the integration of the distorted body image and a relinquishing of the object world in favor of the person's own body. The result must be a severely restricted relationship to the external world and to objects. The extent to which such an outcome is a possibility for these adolescents may be indicated by the absence of outward signs of hatred or rejection of the sexual body (signs of self-injury, suicidal impulses, neglect of the body). From the point of view of assessment the absence of such signs implies that there is no longer an ongoing struggle forcing the adolescent to reject or punish his sexual body; instead he has already accepted his distorted body image.

But the ability to obtain gratification from sublimatory activities assumes a special importance for adolescents whose link with reality is tenuous. The adolescent who is showing signs of psychotic functioning but who is able to make use of sublimatory activities is protected from feeling totally dependent on his body for gratification; this affords some measure of relief from the anxiety that his sexual body forces him to experience.

What part, if any, do we attribute to potentially traumatic real events that occur during adolescence? We have in mind particular events such as illness or death, separation or divorce of parents, re-marriage of a parent, pregnancy of the adolescent, or long pe-riods of unemployment of a parent or of the adolescent.

A constant and predictable "external world"—relationship to each of the parents, to siblings, and to people who form the ex-tended family—acts as an auxiliary ego for the adolescent and helps him cope with the anxiety evoked by developmental con-flicts. The adolescent who has experienced a developmental breakdown is, however, especially vulnerable to changes in his external world, which represent failure of one or both oedipal objects.

One potentially harmful effect of a traumatic real event on the adolescent's development is due to the added anxiety aroused in the move toward establishing the identification with the parent of the same sex. We are aware of the impact of guilt, shame, anger, and depression on the adolescent, but these themselves do not damage the adolescent's development if the response is primarily a reaction to the traumatic event. But if there is uncertainty or doubt about the identification with the parent of the same sex, the potentially traumatic real event can have a seriously damaging effect on the outcome of the identi-fication process and therefore on the sexual organization.

Some adolescents who have experienced a developmental breakdown use the external world as a source of stability and as a check on their own psychic distortions. The harm or potential harm of a traumatic real event occurs when the real event con-firms the adolescent's own fantasy, thereby destroying the ex-ternal world's function of helping the adolescent fight some of his own psychic creations. For example, the adolescent's fantasy world may be a sadomasochistic one; if the parents' relation-ship is sadomasochistic and results in a traumatic event such as separation or divorce, it can damage the adolescent's develop-ment and distort his relation to the outside world. Similarly, a parent's physical or mental illness can act as an additional source of serious interference in the adolescent's development if it acts as a confirmation of the adolescent's fantasy about the sadistic or destructive nature of the oedipal relationship and the fantasied reasons for the parent's illness.

How do we distinguish the severity of the present interference and the diagnostic implications (psychotic functioning or development toward psychosis, for example)? The assessment of developmental breakdown does not itself tell us the extent of interference in the adolescent's relation to external reality or whether the breakdown has already resulted or is likely to result in a complete break with reality. Even though it may be extremely difficult to assess the presence of psychotic functioning or a move toward psychosis, this is nevertheless a most critical assessment to make. One difficulty is that, for the adolescent, we cannot and should not use the distinction between neurosis and psychosis as we might for the adult. For the adolescent, the distortion of external reality may contain the projections or externalizations that are part of the struggle going on to try to integrate the new body image. Psychotic functioning in adolescence can have a defensive meaning, which is linked to the ongoing developmental process. What might be psychotic in an adult (paranoid delusions, ideas of reference, hallucinations) can, if transient in the adolescent, represent the intensity of the anxiety aroused by the developmental conflict.

The factors of special importance in the assessment of psychotic functioning or of the vulnerability to psychosis are the direction of the libido (whether it remains object-directed or is mainly narcissistic), the extent of distortion of the sexual body image, the extent of acceptance or rejection of the sexual body, and whether genital sexuality has already been given up. Certain forms of behavior enable us to conclude that the adolescent has the ability to function on a psychotic level, but this itself does not enable us to conclude that the adolescent has moved or will move toward a more acute and permanent break with reality.

Some adolescents believe that they can acquire a different kind of body through certain actions or identifications, and *they*

do not doubt that this is a possibility. The adolescent who lives with the definite belief that, after death, he will acquire that different body (the kind that he has always wanted) would have to be considered as moving toward or as vulnerable to psychosis. This would also be true of the adolescent who is convinced, without doubt, that his ability to reach inner peace and contentment is dependent on the acquisition of a new kind of body (as would be the case with those adolescents who insist that they must have their genitals removed or changed). With those adolescents who seek other forms of body change, either of their own body or the body of their sexual partner (i.e., change in size of breasts, in shape of nose), we have to consider the possibility of the move to psychosis in the future.

There are adolescents whose breakdowns manifest themselves more by withdrawal from objects and whose fantasies about their own sexual bodies and the bodies of others are lived out secretly via their own bodies. For example, the adolescent who isolates himself in his room (even though he may still attend school or keep a job) and who dresses up in clothes of the opposite sex shows, at the least, signs of severe developmental breakdown. If such activity is accompanied by masturbation (with ejaculation or climax) or by sexual excitement, we should see this as a sign of the presence of psychotic functioning (i.e., the development toward perversion), with a possible move toward psychosis. The extent of the defensive quality of the behavior or the extent to which the adolescent is secretly seeking another kind of body, which he feels he must find, can help us to differentiate between psychotic functioning and the possible move toward psychosis later (Freud 1911, 1919; Katan 1950).

Some adolescents live out certain compelling fantasies through their bodies or through their efforts to change the image of their bodies. Their gratification may be intense, but so is their distortion of external reality. For some the existence of a functioning penis or a functioning vagina *as part of one's body* at puberty and during adolescence is experienced as equivalent to a destruction of the defense against accepting his or her sexual body and accompanying body image, resulting in an even greater distortion of reality than might have existed during latency and at the time of the oedipal resolution, and expressed now through delusional constructs or regressions that maintain a fantasied relationship to the oedipal objects whereby perverse fantasies are gratified. But this behavior or distortion of reality may be the means now available of living out a fantasy of the body as being both male and female.

In assessment, the picture presented by the adolescent may be that of someone who has either completely lost his link with reality or behaves in ways meant to change the reality. The adolescent may seem to be deluded or may be in danger of killing or harming that body which he feels is persecuting him and which is now standing in the way of a secret euphoria, or he may physically attack and endanger the oedipal object (or its substitute) as a means of punishing the object for what he feels has been done to him. Puberty and adolescence, for these adolescents, represent a traumatic confrontation with the failure of their defensive efforts of the past either to have both a male-female body *as one* or to have a body of the opposite sex. For them, a more extreme break with reality at puberty or during adolescence is a further defensive effort to maintain the earlier distortions, which contain a rejection of their actual sexual body as their only means of holding on to the fantasy of themselves as something other than what they actually are now.

Such manifestations in adolescence may give the impression of psychosis. The issue, from the point of view of assessment, is whether there are signs of foreclosure of the developmental process, as described earlier, or whether we can still locate any link with reality and any signs of *doubt* about the solutions the adolescent has had to adopt.

But these manifestations of psychosis have to be differentiated from the schizophrenias or other psychoses of adulthood. With the adult, we see a fixed and irreversible sexual body image, a fixed means of dealing with both external and internal reality. To regard the manifestations in adolescence as equivalent to those of adulthood would be a grave error of assessment because it would not be taking into account the distortions due to the developmental process—that is, to the nature and quality of the anxiety experienced as a result of being confronted with a sexually functioning male or female body—or to the possibilities that exist during adolescence of reversing the pathological process. In this area of pathology, there is the greatest risk of misdiagnosis.

We do not think one can or should make the diagnosis in adolescence of established and irreversible psychosis. Instead, when assessing the severity of psychopathology in adolescents who show or have shown signs of a break with reality, we think it is essential to apply categories that take into account the impact of the developmental process on the defensive process and on the fantasies. We make use of the following categories: 1) psychotic episode, 2) psychotic functioning, and 3) ongoing psychotic process. For the adolescent who has experienced a *psychotic episode* (suicide attempt, self-mutilation), there is a temporary break with reality. He repudiates or denies a part of external reality as a means of negating the source of his internal pain. For the adolescent who presents areas of *psychotic functioning* (anorexia, obesity, drug taking or addiction, severe depression), there is a distortion of reality through projection, but the internalized oedipal objects are themselves experienced as the persecutors who are now kept under control by controlling the feelings and fantasies coming from his own body. The assessment of an *ongoing psychotic process* should be reserved for a special category of disorder in adolescence. Although the psychotic process may, by the end of adolescence, appear to have become established, we do not think that such an outcome is inevitable. Such a process may be initiated as the result of the breakdown at puberty, and the malignant process may be strengthened by factors that encourage the continued distortion of reality and act as a constant force against any change taking place in the adolescent's relationship to his sexual body. As he moves into adulthood, that is, at the time when his final sexual organization is established, the various distortions (his perception of reality; his image of his own body) can become organized into a psychotic illness.

13
The Work of Assessment

The analyst's view of the function of assessment and of his part in enabling the adolescent to understand what is wrong is important in the success or failure of the assessment process. Assessment means judgment and prediction. It implies knowing what to take seriously and when to be concerned and knowing how to listen to what the adolescent is saying. The experience of assessment for the adolescent need not rely on the special ability of one analyst or another to engage him; the application of what we know about adolescent disorders and the anxieties attached to them can enable us to encourage the adolescent to take an active part in the assessment process without feeling that we may harm him if we allow him to know what is going on. There is a vast difference between making use of the assessment procedure and expecting or demanding that the adolescent tell us everything. From our experience, most adolescents who are sent or come for help are relieved if their emotional state is taken seriously, even if this increases their anxiety about the extent of their abnormality. For them, it is essential to feel that their anxieties and fears have been acknowledged and understood and that their concerns about themselves have not been dismissed or misunderstood.

THE AIM AND FUNCTION OF ASSESSMENT

Although the primary aim of assessment can be defined as establishing what is wrong, the whole procedure of being interviewed and encouraged to talk about himself can be a very important experience in the adolescent's life. Every adolescent whom we have interviewed for assessment has come with the fear that something is wrong with him. It is important for his own relation to his internal life and for his view of what can be done to help him that we try to remove the bewilderment and the frightening magic of "assessing."

It is, for example, appropriate to explain why a question has been asked and what we will do with the answer. The adolescent should also begin to understand, through our explanation of what we are doing and why, how we go about deciding what may be wrong and what can be done to help. This may seem to be a seductive procedure, but it need not be so if the interviewer conveys his awareness of the adolescent's anxiety. Many adolescents who come for help have never before talked to anyone about their problems nor acknowledged consciously the extent to which they have been and are burdened by what they believe is wrong with them. When the interviewer and the adolescent jointly formulate what is wrong, the frightening unknown becomes a little less powerful, and at the same time the adolescent may begin to feel some hope that someone understands what is wrong and may be able to help.

If the adolescent is not too hampered by the anxiety he brings with him to the interviews, it is of great use for assessment to scan his whole present life—his social relationships, his schooling or work, the relationship with his parents, his plans for the future. The primary function of assessment is to establish the severity of the present crisis, which has made the adolescent seek help, and to define the extent of interference in the developmental process. This will help us define whether a breakdown took place at puberty and link the present crisis to the resulting interference in development. A difficulty that may occur is that the information we need to make such a link may not be available to us or to the adolescent except through treatment. Nevertheless, there may still be ways open to us during the assessment period to learn from the adolescent about what actually happened at puberty and during his adolescence.

Our own bias in assessment is to try to understand the nature of the adolescent's relationship to his own body and to establish the quality and direction of the central sexual identifications

that exist. We will want to know how the adolescent is responding to the fact that his body is now physically mature. In
optimal circumstances, we may be able to get such information
from the adolescent's description of his relationships to people
of the same or the opposite sex, from a description of his masturbation activity (including his masturbation fantasies), and
generally from the way in which he takes care of his body. The
details of the adolescent's relationship to his own sexual body
will contain information about the quality of the aggression directed against it. This can be one of the main means of establishing the extent of interference in the developmental process.
It is also one of the means of establishing the severity of the
breakdown which may have taken place at puberty and its
cumulative effect on the adolescent's present life—especially
whether it contains ingredients that put his life at risk or might
cause him to move toward psychotic or perverse functioning
and later psychosis.

Bob, for example, a young man of nineteen, said that he had
been worried about himself for a long time but had not been
able to make himself seek help because he thought the process
might be embarrassing and unpleasant, and in any case he was
not sure that it would be of much use. Recently, however, he
had become very concerned when he realized that while on a
walk he went to a nearby railway station, and he had thought
of killing himself. He had suddenly decided against it because
he had told his parents he would never do such a thing. He was
dressed shabbily, he kept glancing away, and he giggled and
blushed when he talked of this incident. The analyst's first impression was of a very disturbed person. He started the interview by saying that Bob had looked worried when he entered
the consulting room, and he had wondered whether Bob had
been concerned about what he might want to discuss. Bob's
first response suggested that Bob's pathology, although severe,
might be less ominous than the analyst had initially assumed
from his appearance. Bob said that he had felt troubled for
years; he had nearly given up, but he had come because he
hoped that the analyst might be able to do something for him.
He talked of his loneliness, of his difficulty in having a

girlfriend, of his sudden failure at school after a long record as one of the best in the school, and of his feeling of failure because he was working as a clerk after he, his family, and his teachers had all assumed that he would go to a leading university. The analyst acknowledged the feeling of failure Bob must be having to live with, as well as the shame and anger with himself and the hopelessness.

Bob could then begin to talk about his masturbation activity, making it easier to understand why he presented such a disorganized and shabby picture of himself. It was also possible to decide that the pathological process was not a psychotic one, even though it reflected the presence of severe interference in functioning. He talked of his long-standing inability to touch his penis, of his humiliation when he could masturbate only by using a vibrator, and of his belief that he was irreversibly abnormal. He was able to describe the extent of the worry about himself; there was no evidence of a belief in or concern about ominous body changes or of experiencing weird feelings from his body, which would have implied a more psychotic process. In telling the analyst all this, Bob stared at him to see how he responded. With some encouragement from the analyst, Bob was able to say that he thought the analyst might be disgusted and would think of Bob as a pervert.

Bob was very much in touch with his anxiety and with the extent of his isolation. That the problem was an internal one had clearly been accepted by Bob before he sought help, and the question of his need for help was not difficult to discuss with him. But before the question of help could be discussed, the analyst had to assure himself that what Bob had told him represented what he believed to be true and that he was not keeping from the analyst facts or feelings that might change the assessment or add an element of urgency or risk to the picture. When Bob talked of his past hopelessness, he said that he had thought of killing himself, but he felt he could not do such a thing to his parents. This could be understood by the analyst as meaning that the relationship to his internal parents had not been destroyed and that in seeking some way of doing something about himself he was also wanting to restore his relationship to them. This, at least temporarily, seemed to rule out immediate danger to his life. Although a developmental breakdown must have taken place and was now expressing itself through isolation, academic failure, and the form taken by his sexual life—the use of the vibrator could be understood as a way of needing to remain passive in his masturbation activity—there did not seem to be the ingredients of a break with reality or a more permanent distortion of his image of his own body.

The analyst encouraged Bob to take his disturbance seriously even if it did not mean that he was a pervert, as had been his fear. He could tell Bob that without help he would very likely begin to hate his body because of his feeling of failing sexually; he could also make the link to Bob's present severe depression. The danger of leaving Bob's depression untreated was of a more permanent withdrawal with increased suspiciousness and a more organized paranoid structure in early adult life. Although there was no blaming of others and no sign of fixed paranoid ideas, Bob's present sexual life contained the repeated destruction of himself as a potent male.

THE HIDDEN-URGENT PROBLEMS

There is a group of adolescents who present special problems of assessment, who may from a practical point of view be in urgent need of help of some kind, but whose depression makes it very difficult to get in touch with the urgency of the problem. These adolescents also say they are worried, but they do not quite know why. They come without any sense of having reached a crisis in their lives. In describing their day-to-day lives as well as their immediate past, they create a picture of suffering or despair that contains a pervasive feeling that everything is worthless or hopeless. This holds true not just for severely depressed adolescents but for those in particular who feel that nothing has changed for years and that nothing can ever change. The depression of these adolescents is in fact characterized by the feeling that there is no possibility of something altering in their lives. Nevertheless, they have not given up completely but often have come for assessment thinking that this is a last try. The problems these adolescents present are hidden from themselves, and the urgency is something they are not at all aware of when they first seek help. With these adolescents the analyst can easily miss the severity of the existing pathology or the impending danger to their lives especially if they feel that their "last try" has resulted in failure. An important function of the analyst is to make conscious the extent of their desperation and the risk to their lives if they feel that all has failed.

Breakdown

The feelings of worthlessness or hopelessness in these adolescents are always a result of something that was experienced and usually repressed earlier in adolescence—an experience that at the time bewildered and terrified them. They thought they either were mad or might go mad; they felt disorganized by their uncontrollable regressive thoughts or compulsive actions—thoughts or actions that were directly linked to the feelings coming from their sexually mature bodies. When seen for assessment, some of these adolescents describe themselves as dead, not caring, feeling hopeless, hating themselves, and not knowing what to do with themselves, but without any awareness that they have given up yet already seeing themselves as abnormal or as having failed.

In such instances the assessment serves a function that goes beyond eliciting the information needed to understand the severity of the pathology. The assessment interviews can be used very effectively to enable the adolescent to try again to come into touch with the anxiety that at one time overwhelmed him. More specifically, the mere act of putting into words his despair, his shame, his feeling of responsibility for his thoughts or actions, and his wish simply to give up can be a highly significant step forward. In the assessment interviews it is often not possible for us to determine what these thoughts really are about or to what extent the interference that is present is of a secondary nature. During the assessment it is of the utmost importance to establish whether a developmental breakdown took

place at puberty—that is, whether there had been an experience of being overwhelmed by the belief of having lost control
of the ability to do anything about their feelings or actions.
These adolescents recall the breakdown as a time when they
temporarily lost the link with reality—*and it is this that terrified
them.*

We have discussed earlier why we believe that a breakdown
regularly occurs at puberty in adolescents who attempt suicide
and that a state of deadlock exists in the developmental process.[1] Adolescents who have attempted suicide present a special problem of assessment and management—to which we will
return. Less obvious and less clear signs of a breakdown in
functioning are seen in those adolescents who slowly withdraw
from the outside world, who drift into drug use and then become dependent on drugs and unable to risk giving them up
("Why should I be mad and empty when I can feel that I have
friends?" or "It's lovely, the penis shrinks, and it's almost impossible to get an erection—but it doesn't matter, because at
times like that you don't need a penis."), or who adopt beliefs
or behavior that make them totally ascetic.[2] These adolescents
may be viewed wrongly as making use of normal adolescent defensive maneuvers; they are often described as neurotic or ec-
centric. But such descriptions help deny the severity of the disturbance that may be present and the extent to which nothing
has changed in these people's lives from early adolescence on.

Helen, aged nineteen, explained that she could not concentrate. She had been thinking of seeking help for some time, but
she decided to do something about her difficulties when she realized that she was refusing time after time to accept invitations
from boys to go to parties. Instead, on Saturday evenings, she
would read, listen to records, and then just go to sleep. Once
when she did go out with a boy and he tried to kiss her, she felt
disgusted and had to spend a long time when she came home
washing her face and looking in the mirror to see that there

1. See chapter 8.
2. See chapter 1.

was nothing unusual about her looks. She was aware that this behavior was ridiculous, but she had to do it. At present she did not have many friends—she preferred to spend her time alone.

In response to questions during interviews, she described how she hated herself when she first began to menstruate, how she cried and felt that her father would never love her again as he used to. Instead of saying anything that might help her to see what the conflict was about, the analyst said that this must have been an awful time for her and wondered also whether she continued to have trouble about menstruation. With much embarrassment, she said that her periods had been irregular for four or five years, but now they were all right. After the analyst explained why he wanted to know about these things, Helen went on to talk about her isolation, the thoughts of suicide which had haunted her for some years, and her feeling that something had happened to her, which left her with the idea that part of her mind was detached from the rest of her.

She had already given the analyst a number of signals that something had indeed gone wrong earlier in her adolescence, and when she was asked to describe further her feeling of disgust when the boy tried to kiss her, she casually talked about her eating difficulties in the past. These turned out to be anorexia nervosa; perhaps a better description would be compulsive fasting. At the age of seventeen her weight had dropped from 115 to 70 pounds; it was a time when she felt fine because her body was dead and she knew that she was weak and ugly. She had almost no feelings, so there was nothing to be worried about. The analyst responded by saying, "You were very right to have come. You've been very unhappy for a long time, but you couldn't do anything about it until now because you were too ashamed. But now that you have come for help, you *must* do something about your life." This experience was very important for Helen. Not only could the analyst recognize that her past difficulties were, in fact, an illness, but it was possible to convey to her that she could be helped and that some change could take place. It was as if she now had an ally in her

fight against something that until then had simply been terrifying to her.

Adolescents Whose Lives Are At Risk

The other group of adolescents who have hidden-urgent problems are those who have attempted suicide or whose self-
hatred and depression are so severe that they become convinced
that there is no answer to their plight because they are unable
to feel that they deserve to live.

It is not at all uncommon that the actual suicide attempt took
place some time prior to their seeking help, and often we learn
about it only in response to our questioning rather than because the adolescent freely tells us about it. It is also remark-
able how often such information is not given to us either by the
parents or by professional people (if they are the ones who are
first in touch with us). We may be told that the adolescent is
feeling depressed or does not want to work or is behaving in an
odd way, but very often there is no reference to a previous suicide attempt.

Even though the adolescent may say that now everything is
fine and that what he is really worried about is his job or not
having a girlfriend or feeling sexually abnormal, we react to
the information of a past suicide attempt as if it is an urgent
crisis, *no matter when the attempt was made.* To have tried to kill
himself means that there is, in fantasy, a part of him that is
dead and to which he maintains a relationship. We make it
quite clear to the adolescent that we see his suicide attempt as a
past or present sign of illness and why we think so. We always
let him know that we think he is still at risk of repeating it.

From a management or practical point of view, we always involve the parents of the adolescent who attempted suicide, conveying to them as well our view of the seriousness of the situation. Of course, some of the adolescents and parents think we
are making a fuss about nothing, and they try to dismiss what
we say. But from our experience with the psychoanalytic treatment of adolescents who have attempted suicide, as well as that
of colleagues who have analyzed such adolescents, we are convinced that from an assessment and practical point of view it is

correct to consider such an event an urgent crisis and to make it into a family crisis.[3] To do less than this is to deny the power of the omnipotent fantasy which may temporarily be kept under control but which can, under certain precipitating circumstances, seriously interfere with the adolescent's reality-testing function and result in another suicide attempt.

There are other adolescents whose lives are seriously at risk even though they have not previously attempted suicide. Their belief in their worthlessness is pervasive, and they live with the conviction that there is nothing good in them or that they are irreversibly sexually abnormal. Their self-hatred has been with them for years and becomes extreme at puberty, often now being directed at their bodies. In their relationships they feel forced to get people to behave toward them in ways that will confirm their worthlessness.

It is not at all an uncommon feature for these adolescents to be *compelled* to carry out certain actions that will result in damage to their bodies or will endanger their lives. These actions are often devoid of conscious fantasy content, but the adolescent experiences their power as autonomous and extremely powerful. We have in mind such actions as self-cutting or various dangerous activities, for example, constantly being alone in certain places. (In assessment, the issue is not only whether the compelling need to put certain thoughts into action is present. It is critical to try to establish whether being "compelled" is based on a fantasy of hatred, need for punishment, need for certain kinds of sexual gratification, or whether this compelling quality contains ingredients that are the precursors of hallucinations or delusions—that is, of being ordered to act or of having to do something because the internal persecutor's voice is being heard.)

Rebecca, aged seventeen, had to be interviewed over an extended period of time because she was silent for the first three meetings and then spoke very little and with caution. But she gave the analyst a number of clues which made it possible for her to talk to the girl and, in this way, to counter Rebecca's sus-

3. See chapters 8 and 9.

picion and extreme shame. The analyst talked of Rebecca's being very sad, of her finding it difficult to look at the analyst,
and of her thinking that there was little to live for. It was only
when the analyst promised Rebecca that she would try to help
her no matter what she told the analyst that Rebecca cried and
began to talk.

She wanted to be dead because she felt sexually abnormal
and because she knew there was no hope. She spent her time
eating (she was very much overweight) and reading. She felt
she had to ride her motorcycle late every night at very high
speeds and had recently been involved in a number of near-
misses. Sometimes she cut her arms with a razor. She did not
hear voices, nor did she feel ordered to do things; she thought
it was more the case that she needed to do such things whenever she overate. She refused to trust anybody now—a girl she
liked had disappeared, and a man she liked had tricked her
into having intercourse with him and then never contacted her
again. When she thought of being dead she realized she did
not think of anybody—it was as if she had already killed the
people who might have cared, and she then felt empty and
completely worthless. This emphasized to the analyst that the
situation was critical. Rebecca said that since she had been able
to mention these problems for the first time, she had begun to
feel just a little hope. But she ran out of the room when the analyst said something in the next interview that frightened her.
The analyst wrote to her saying that she should return because
she needed to come, reminding her of the promise made earlier that the analyst would try to help. When Rebecca returned,
she told the analyst that, by writing, the analyst had done something that Rebecca never believed would be done for her by
anybody. Rebecca was expressing her belief that nobody could
ever again make her feel that she was worth anything, but the
letter had changed that attitude a little.

With Rebecca it was essential for the analyst to act temporarily as if she were talking on behalf of Rebecca and to find
words that Rebecca herself could not allow herself to use. She
was terrified of something unknown, but there were sufficient
clues to conclude that her worthlessness and self-hatred never

allowed any respite. That Rebecca felt compelled to carry out certain actions enabled the analyst to express some of the meaning of Rebecca's anxiety about her madness and hopelessness. But it also conveyed how powerless Rebecca felt at this point and why she often preferred to be dead. The concentration on what Rebecca was experiencing now—her self-hatred, her fear of becoming a lesbian, her relentless need to attack her body, and her ability to take part in adding new meaning to her "mad behavior"—made it possible for the assessment process to proceed. At first, being helped meant to Rebecca being able to talk with the analyst and finding some additional hope. But the analyst's continued use of the interviews in a therapeutic fashion and her ready expression of concern about Rebecca's vulnerability allowed the assessment data to be obtained as she simultaneously prepared Rebecca for urgent treatment.

SETTING UP THE FRAMEWORK FOR TREATMENT

We address ourselves to the issue of the framework for treatment—plans, arrangements, preparation, undertakings—because of the need to take into account the possibility that various crises may arise that must affect the adolescent's daily life, and, if not dealt with, that could easily jeopardize the future of the treatment. Some analysts may arrange for treatment on the assumption that the framework will unfold as treatment progresses. This often does not work. Setting up the framework for treatment can be considered to be part of the assessment process, and time should be allowed to help the adolescent and, when necessary, his parents understand its purpose.

Throughout the assessment process, the interviews can be used to help the adolescent become more familiar with the meaning and possible expectations of treatment. Adolescents may agree to treatment without knowing or questioning what is wrong and what the treatment is for and may instead think either secretly or passively that the analyst will "cure" them or will confirm that they are beyond help. The submission to the analyst's authority and to the treatment may initially make for an easy time but ultimately can be an important factor in the failure of the treatment.

The extent of the framework that is needed will be determined primarily by the analyst's assessment of the severity of the breakdown at puberty and the manner in which defensive functioning or deadlock indicates that there is a crisis in the adolescent's present life. We have to take into account such factors as the adolescent's ability to function at present—that is, to attend school or carry on with his work—and also whether there is a history of self-destructive actions and, if so, whether the adolescent's life is now at risk. These are urgent or potentially urgent issues and should be discussed and planned for during the preparation for treatment. It may even be necessary to continue to see the adolescent over a period of time as part of a prolonged assessment in order to allow the present crisis to be worked through before undertaking an actual commitment to treatment. But beyond these issues, there is no need for any special arrangements or commitments to be considered by the adolescent or his parents.

The analyst's recognition of the presence of developmental deadlock or illness requires, at the same time, the readiness to deal with the consequences of his decision and of his recommendations. It is not unusual for the analyst to want to compromise with what he believes to be essential and to wait and see. There may be times when the adolescent's present plans have to be disrupted and his present life made more difficult by the demands and expectations of treatment. We do not advocate stringent or extreme measures or arrangements, but if the present consequences of the developmental breakdown are severe, and there are risks to the adolescent's life or to his psychological future, it may be necessary to discuss with him and his parents some definite undertakings, even if these seriously affect the adolescent's present plans for school or work.

The adolescent must be able to take part in the decisions about the various undertakings—that is, he should understand what is being discussed and why and the meaning of certain arrangements or commitments. It is necessary for him to acknowledge that he is in need of treatment, that the arrangements are part of the analyst's recognition that he is at risk or ill, and that the analyst's commitment to helping him work toward change can be carried out only within a certain context. It is also important to convey to the adolescent and his family that the treatment being recommended and the person carrying out the treatment require a certain framework, and that in situations of crisis it is likely that the power of the illness will be much greater than the power of the analyst. But it is also necessary, before treatment begins, that the person making the arrangements and the person carrying out the treatment (if these are different people) are themselves clear about what is needed. In other words, it is advisable that the analyst try to convey that carrying out the treatment is the responsibility of the analyst and that he needs a certain framework for this to be possible.

The framework for the treatment may have to include the following:

1. *Recommendation for Treatment*
   The adolescent should know why one form of treatment or another is being recommended, what this implies regarding attendance and frequency, and why this form of treatment has been chosen over any other. Where the adolescent's present academic or work life will be disrupted, or when there is or may be a risk to the adolescent's life, the parents must be included in these discussions and arrangements, and they should agree with what is being decided before any treatment is begun.
2. *School, Work, and Use of Available Time*
   If the adolescent is not able to attend school or work at present, it should be clarified what he will do during the day, who will be available to him, and how he will spend his time. It is usually detrimental to the progress of the treatment for the adolescent to be unoccupied throughout the day.
3. *Where the Adolescent Will Live*
   In most circumstances, this is not a serious issue, but it becomes one in those instances where there have been self-de-

structive acts, where the adolescent's life has been or is at
risk, or where there has been a history of psychotic functioning. In such circumstances, arrangements should be
made with the parents for the adolescent not to be left alone
for any length of time—for example, on weekends or during vacations. This means that the adolescent should not live
alone and that any change in his living arrangements should
be discussed with the analyst.

4. *Adolescents Who May Require Hospital Care*

If the adolescent is now or should be in the hospital, arrangements should be made with the hospital for him to be
discharged only with the prior agreement of the analyst who
is carrying out the treatment. Similarly, arrangements
should be made for his readmission if this is required during the treatment period. Although it is often difficult to establish these arrangements with a hospital, it is nevertheless
advisable to address such an eventuality.

We are aware that the framework for treatment itself does
not bring us closer to an understanding of the meaning of the
adolescent's present disorder. But with the development of the
transference, and especially of the transference breakdown as
part of the undoing of the pathology, we are often faced with
serious crises that require a combination of understanding and
a recognition of the practical and immediate problems in the
adolescent's life.[4] The framework for treatment can be an essential ally and should form part of the total contact with the
adolescent during the assessment process.

4. See chapter 6.

References

Abraham, K. (1924). A short study of the development of the libido, viewed in the light of mental disorders. In *Selected Papers of Karl Abraham*. London: Hogarth Press, 1949, pp. 418–501.

Adatto, C. P. (1966). On the metamorphosis from adolescence into adulthood. *J. Amer. Psychoanal. Assn.* 14: 485–509.

Aichhorn, A. (1925). *Wayward Youth*. London: Imago, 1951.

Arlow, J. A. (1953). Masturbation and symptom formation. *J. Amer. Psychoanal. Assn.* 1: 45–58.

Bak, R. C. (1939). Regression of ego-orientation and libido in schizophrenia. *Int. J. Psychoanal.* 20: 64–71.

Bender, L. (1959). The concept of pseudopsychopathic schizophrenia in adolescents. *Am. J. Orthopsychiat.* 29: 491–509.

Beres, D. (1956). Ego deviation and the concept of schizophrenia. *Psychoanal. Study Child* 11: 164–235.

——— & Obers, S. J. (1950). The effects of extreme deprivation in infancy on psychic structure in adolescence: a study in ego development. *Psychoanal. Study Child* 5: 212–35.

Bernfeld, S. (1923). Über eine typische form der männlichen pubertät. *Imaqo* 9: 169–88.

——— (1938). Types of adolescence. *Psychoanal. Q.* 7: 243–53.

Bibring, G. L. (1959). Some considerations of the psychological processes in pregnancy. *Psychoanal. Study Child* 14: 113–21.

Blos, P. (1954). Prolonged adolescence. *Am. J. Orthopsychiat.* 24: 733–42.

——— (1962). *On Adolescence*. New York: Free Press.

——— (1966). The concept of acting out in relation to the adolescent process. In *A Developmental Approach to Problems of Acting Out*, ed. E. Rexford. New York: Int. Univ. Press, pp. 153–82.

——— (1967). The second individuation process of adolescence. *Psychoanal. Study Child* 22: 162–86.

———— (1972). The epigenesis of the adult neurosis. *Psychoanal. Study Child* 27: 106–35.

———— (1977). When and how does adolescence end: structural criteria for adolescent closure. *Adolescent Psychiatry* 5: 5–17.

Bruch, H. (1977). Anorexia Nervosa. *Adolescent Psychiatry* 5: 293–303.

Brunswick, R. M. (1940). The pre-oedipal phase of the libido development. *Psychoanal. Q.* 9: 293–319.

Buxbaum, E. (1958). Panel report: the psychology of adolescence. *J. Amer. Psychoanal. Assn.* 6: 111–20.

Chasseguet-Smirgel, J. (1981). Loss of reality in perversions—with special reference to fetishism. *J. Amer. Psychoanal. Assn.* 29, 511–34.

Clower, V. L. (1975). Significance of masturbation in female sexual development and function. In *Masturbation*, ed. I. M. Marcus & J. J. Francis. New York: Int. Univ. Press, pp. 107–44.

Dewald, P. A. (1978). The psychoanalytic process in adult patients. *Psychoanal. Study Child* 33: 323–32.

Deutsch, H. (1932). On female homosexuality. *Psychoanal. Q.* 1: 484–510.

———— (1942). Some forms of emotional disturbance and their relationship to schizophrenia. *Psychoanal. Q.* 11: 301–21.

———— (1944). *The Psychology of Women*, vol. 1. New York: Grune & Stratton.

———— (1945). *The Psychology of Women*, vol. 2. New York: Grune & Stratton.

———— (1968). *Selected Problems of Adolescence*. New York: Int. Univ. Press.

Dibble, E. D. & Cohen, D. J. (1981). Personality development in identical twins: the first decade of life. *Psychoanal. Study Child* 36: 45–70.

Eissler, K. R. (1958). Notes on problems of technique in the psychoanalytic treatment of adolescents: with special remarks on perversions. *Psychoanal. Study Child* 13: 223–54.

Ekstein R. (1978). The process of termination and its relation to outcome in the treatment of psychotic disorders in adolescence. *Adolescent Psychiatry* 6: 448–60.

Erikson, E. H. (1956). The problem of ego identity. *J. Amer. Psychoanal. Assn.* 4: 56–121.

———— (1959). *Identity and the Life Cycle. Psychological Issues*, mono. 1. New York: Int. Univ. Press.

Erlich, H. S. (1978). Adolescent suicide: maternal longing and cognitive development. *Psychoanal. Study Child* 33: 261–77.

Esman, A. H. (1973). The primal scene: a review and a reconsideration. *Psychoanal. Study Child* 28: 49–81.

Federn, P. (1952). *Ego Psychology and the Psychoses*. New York: Basic.

Feigelson, C. I. (1976). Reconstruction of adolescence (and early latency) in the analysis of an adult woman. *Psychoanal. Study Child* 31: 225–36.

Ferenczi, S. (1911). On the part played by homosexuality in the pathogenesis of paranoia. In *Sex in Psychoanalysis*. New York: Basic, 1950, pp. 154–86.

—— (1913). Stages in the development of the sense of reality. In *First Contributions to Psycho-Analysis*. London: Hogarth Press, 1952, pp. 213–39.

Francis, J. J. (1968). Panel report: masturbation. *J. Amer. Psychoanal. Assn.* 16: 95–112.

—— & Marcus, I. M. (1975). Masturbation: a developmental view. In *Masturbation*, ed. I. M. Marcus & J. J. Francis. New York: Int. Univ. Press, pp. 9–52.

Freud, A. (1937). *The Ego and the Mechanisms of Defence*. London: Hogarth Press.

—— (1949). Aggression in relation to emotional development: normal and pathological. *Psychoanal. Study Child* 3/4: 37–48.

—— (1952). A connection between the states of negativism and of emotional surrender. *Int. J. Psychoanal.* 33: 265 (abstract).

—— (1958). Adolescence. *Psychoanal. Study Child* 13: 255–78.

—— (1965). *Normality and Pathology in Childhood*. New York: Int. Univ. Press.

—— (1968). Acting out. *Int. J. Psychoanal.* 49: 165–70.

Freud, S. (1892–1899). Extracts from the Fliess letters. *S.E.* 1: 173–280.

—— (1905). Fragment of an analysis of a case of hysteria. *S.E.* 7: 3–122.

—— (1905). Three essays on the theory of sexuality. *S.E.* 7: 125–243.

—— (1906). My views on the part played by sexuality in the aetiology of the neuroses. *S.E.* 7: 271–79.

—— (1910). Contributions to a discussion on suicide. *S.E.* 11: 231–32.

—— (1911). Psycho-analytic notes on an autobiographical account of a case of paranoia (dementia paranoides). *S.E.* 12: 3–82.

—— (1914). On narcissism: an introduction. *S.E.* 14: 69–102.

—— (1914). Remembering, repeating and working-through. *S.E.* 12: 145–56.

—— (1917). Mourning and melancholia. *S.E.* 14: 239–58.

—— (1919). A child is being beaten. *S.E.* 17: 177–204.

—— (1920). Beyond the pleasure principle. *S.E.* 18: 3–64.

—— (1923). The ego and the id. *S.E.* 19: 3–66.

—— (1924). Neurosis and psychosis. *S.E.* 19:149–53.

—— (1924). The dissolution of the Oedipus complex. *S.E.* 19: 173–79.

—— (1924). The loss of reality in neurosis and psychosis. *S.E.* 19: 183–87.

—— (1931). Female sexuality. *S.E.* 21: 223–43.

—— (1937). Constructions in analysis. *S.E.* 23: 255–69.

Friedman, M., Glasser, M., Laufer, E., Laufer, M. & Wohl, M. (1972). Attempted suicide and self-mutilation in adolescence: some observations from a psychoanalytic research project. *Int. J. Psychoanal.* 53: 179–83.

Galenson, E. & Roiphe, H. (1980). The preoedipal development of the boy. *J. Amer. Psychoanal. Assn.* 28: 805–27.

Geleerd, E. R. (1957). Some aspects of psychoanalytic technique in adolescence. *Psychoanal. Study Child* 12: 263–83.

—— (1961). Some aspects of ego vicissitudes in adolescence. *J. Amer. Psychoanal. Assn.* 9: 394–405.

Gillespie, W.H. (1964). Symposium on homosexuality. *Int. J. Psychoanal.* 45: 203–09.

Glover, E. (1933). The relation of perversion formation to the development of reality sense. *Int. J. Psychoanal.* 14: 486–97.

Greenacre, P. (1953). Certain relationships between fetishism and the faulty development of the body image. *Psychoanal. Study Child* 8: 79–98.

—— (1958). Early physical determinants in the development of the sense of identity. *J. Amer. Psychoanal. Assn.* 6: 612–27.

—— (1960). Further notes on fetishism. *Psychoanal. Study Child* 15: 191–207.

—— (1969). The fetish and the transitional object. *Psychoanal. Study Child* 24: 144–64.

—— (1975). On reconstruction. *J. Amer. Psychoanal. Assn.*, 23: 693–712.

Greenson, R. R. (1968). Dis-identifying from mother. *Int. J. Psychoanal.* 49: 370–74.

Gurwitt, A. R. (1976). Aspects of prospective fatherhood: a case report. *Psychoanal. Study Child* 31: 237–71.

Hall, G. S. (1916). *Adolescence*. 2 vols. New York: Appleton.

Harley, M. (1961). Some observations on the relationship between genitality and structural development at adolescence. *J. Amer. Psychoanal. Assn.* 9: 434–60.

——— (1970). On some problems of technique in the analysis of early adolescents. *Psychoanal. Study Child* 25: 99–121.

Hartmann, H. (1953). Contribution to the metapsychology of schizophrenia. *Psychoanal. Study Child* 8: 177–98.

Hoffer, W. (1949). Mouth, hand and ego-integration. *Psychoanal. Study Child* 3/4: 49–56.

——— (1950). Development of the body ego. *Psychoanal. Study Child* 5: 18–24.

Hollender, M. H. (1975). Women's use of fantasy during sexual intercourse. In *Masturbation*, ed. I. M. Marcus & J. J. Francis. New York: Int. Univ. Press, pp. 315–28.

Horney, K. (1933). The denial of the vagina: a contribution to the problem of the genital anxieties specific to women. *Int. J. Psychoanal.* 14: 57–70.

Jacobson, E. (1954). Contribution to the metapsychology of psychotic identifications. *J. Amer. Psychoanal. Assn.* 2: 239–62.

——— (1961). Adolescent moods and the remodeling of psychic structures in adolescence. *Psychoanal. Study Child* 16:164–83.

——— (1964). *The Self and the Object World*. New York: Int. Univ. Press.

——— (1971). *Depression*. New York: Int. Univ. Press.

Jones, E. (1922). Some problems of adolescence. In *Papers on Psycho-Analysis*. London: Ballière, Tindall & Cox, 1948, pp. 389–406.

——— (1927). The early development of female sexuality. In *Papers on Psycho-Analysis*. London: Ballière, Tindall & Cox, 1948, pp. 438–51.

——— (1932). The phallic phase. In *Papers on Psycho-Analysis*. London: Ballière, Tindall & Cox, 1948, pp. 452–84.

——— (1954, 1955, 1957). *Sigmund Freud—Life and Work*. 3 vols. London: Hogarth Press.

Katan, M. (1950). Structural aspects of a case of schizophrenia. *Psychoanal. Study Child* 5: 175–211.

——— (1954). The importance of the non-psychotic part of the personality in schizophrenia. *Int. J. Psychoanal.* 35: 119–28.

—— (1969). A psychoanalytic approach to the diagnosis of paranoia. *Psychoanal. Study Child* 24: 328–57.

—— (1975). Childhood memories as contents of schizophrenic hallucinations and delusions. *Psychoanal. Study Child* 30: 357–74.

Kernberg, O. F. (1979). The contributions of Edith Jacobson: an overview. *J. Amer. Psychoanal. Assn.* 27: 793–819.

—— (1980). Developmental theory, structural organization and psychoanalytic technique. In *Rapprochement*, ed. R. Lax, S. Bach, & J. A. Burland. New York: Aronson, pp. 23–38.

Klein, M. (1928). Early stages of the Oedipus complex. In *Contributions to Psycho-Analysis 1921–1945*. London: Hogarth Press, 1948, pp. 202–14.

—— (1945). The Oedipus complex in the light of early anxieties. In *Contributions to Psycho-Analysis 1921–1945*. London: Hogarth Press, 1948, pp. 339–90.

—— (1958). On the development of mental functioning. *Int. J. Psychoanal.* 39: 84–90.

Klumpner, G. H. (1978). A review of Freud's writings on adolescence. *Adolescent Psychiatry* 6: 59–74.

Kramer, P. (1954). Early capacity for orgastic discharge and character formation. *Psychoanal. Study Child* 9: 128–41.

Kris, E. (1951). Some comments and observations on early autoerotic activities. *Psychoanal. Study Child* 6: 95–116.

—— (1956). The personal myth. *J. Amer. Psychoanal. Assn.* 4: 653–81.

Lampl-de Groot, J. (1950). On masturbation and its influence on general development. *Psychoanal. Study Child* 5: 153–74.

—— (1960). On adolescence. *Psychoanal. Study Child* 15: 95–103.

—— (1962). Ego ideal and superego. *Psychoanal. Study Child* 17: 94–106.

Laufer, M. (1964). Ego ideal and pseudo ego ideal in adolescence. *Psychoanal. Study Child* 19: 196–221.

—— (1968). The body image, the function of masturbation, and adolescence: problems of the ownership of the body. *Psychoanal. Study Child* 23: 114–37.

—— (1976). The central masturbation fantasy, the final sexual organization, and adolescence. *Psychoanal. Study Child* 31: 297–316.

—— (1978). The nature of the adolescent pathology and the psychoanalytic process. *Psychoanal. Study Child* 33: 307–22.

—— (1981). Adolescent breakdown and the transference neurosis. *Int. J. Psychoanal.* 62: 51–59.

———— (1982). The formation and shaping of the Oedipus complex: clinical observations and assumptions. *Int. J. Psychoanal.* 63: 217–27.

Laufer, M. E. (1981). The adolescent's use of the body in object relationships and in the transference: a comparison of borderline and narcissistic modes of functioning. *Psychoanal. Study Child* 36: 163–80.

———— (1982). Female masturbation in adolescence and the development of the relationship to the body. *Int. J. Psychoanal.* 63: 295–302.

Lewin, B. D. (1933). The body as phallus. *Psychoanal. Q.*, 2: 24–47.

———— (1950). *The Psychoanalysis of Elation.* New York: Norton.

Lichtenstein, H. (1961). Identity and Sexuality. *J. Amer. Psychoanal. Assn.* 9: 179–260.

Limentani, A. (1966). A re-evaluation of acting out in relation to working through. *Int. J. Psychoanal.* 47: 274–82.

———— (1977). The differential diagnosis of homosexuality. *Brit. J. Med. Psychol.* 50: 209–16.

Lindner, S. (1879). Das saugen en den fingern, lippen, etc., bei den kindern (ludeln). *Jb. Kinderheilk.*

Little, M. (1958). On delusional transference (transference psychosis). *Int. J. Psychoanal.* 39: 134–38.

Loewald, H. W. (1971). The transference neurosis: comments on the concept and the phenomenon. *J. Amer. Psychoanal. Assn.* 19: 54–66.

———— (1979). The waning of the Oedipus complex. *J. Amer. Psychoanal. Assn.*, 27: 751–75.

Loewenstein, R. M. (1935). Phallic passivity in men. *Int. J. Psychoanal.* 16: 334–40.

Mahler, M. S. (1963). Thoughts about development and individuation. *Psychoanal. Study Child* 18: 307–24.

———— (1974). Symbiosis and individuation: the psychological birth of the human infant. *Psychoanal. Study Child* 29: 89–106.

———— Pine, F. & Bergman, A. (1975). *The Psychological Birth of the Human Infant.* London: Hutchinson.

Marcus, I. M. (1980). Countertransference and the psychoanalytic process in children and adolescents. *Psychoanal. Study Child* 35: 285–98.

Masterson, J. F. (1978). The borderline adolescent: an object relations view. *Adolescent Psychiatry* 6: 344–59.

Milrod, D. (1982). The wished-for self image. *Psychoanal. Study Child* 37: 95–120.

Modell, A. H. (1968). *Object Love and Reality.* New York: Int. Univ. Press.

Mogul, S. L. (1980). Asceticism in adolescence and anorexia nervosa. *Psychoanal. Study Child* 35: 155–75.

Moore, W. T. (1975). Some economic functions of genital masturbation during adolescent development. In *Masturbation*, ed. I. M. Marcus & J. J. Francis. New York: Int. Univ. Press, pp. 231–76.

Peto, A. (1959). Body image and archaic thinking. *Int. J. Psychoanal.* 40: 223–31.

Reich, A. (1951). The discussion of 1912 on masturbation and our present-day views. *Psychoanal. Study Child* 6: 80–94.

———— (1960). Pathologic forms of self-esteem regulation. *Psychoanal. Study Child* 15: 215–32.

Rinsley, D. B. (1981). Borderline psychopathology: the concepts of Masterson and Rinsley and beyond. *Adolescent Psychiatry* 9: 259–74.

Ritvo, S. (1971). Late adolescence: developmental and clinical considerations. *Psychoanal. Study Child* 26: 241–63.

———— (1976). Adolescent to woman. *J. Amer. Psychoanal. Assn.* (supple. 24) 5: 127–38.

———— (1978). The psychoanalytic process in childhood. *Psychoanal. Study Child* 33: 295–305.

———— (1981). Anxiety, symptom formation and ego autonomy. *Psychoanal. Study Child* 36: 339–64.

———— & Solnit, A. J. (1958). Influences of early mother-child interaction on identification processes. *Psychoanal. Study Child* 13: 64–85.

Roiphe, H. (1973). Some thoughts on childhood psychoses, self and object. *Psychoanal. Study Child* 28: 131–45.

Rosenfeld, H. (1964). An investigation into the need of neurotic and psychotic patients to act out during analysis. In *Psychotic States*. New York: Int. Univ. Press, 1966, pp. 200–16.

Sandler, J. (1960). On the concept of superego. *Psychoanal. Study Child* 15: 128–62.

Sands, D. E. (1956). The psychoses of adolescence. In *The Psychology of Adolescence*, ed. A. H. Esman. New York: Int. Univ. Press, 1975, pp. 402–13.

Sarnoff, C. A. (1975). Narcissism, adolescent masturbation fantasies, and the search for reality. In *Masturbation*, ed. I. M. Marcus & J. J. Francis. New York: Int. Univ. Press, pp. 227–304.

Schafer, R. (1960). The loving and beloved superego in Freud's structured theory. *Psychoanal. Study Child* 15: 163–88.

Schilder, P. (1935). *The Image and Appearance of the Human Body*. New York: Intl. Univ. Press, 1950.

Schur, M. (1955). Comments on the metapsychology of somatization. *Psychoanal. Study Child* 10: 119–64.

Segal, H. (1964). *Introduction to the Work of Melanie Klein*. London: W. Heinemann.

———— (1977). Psychoanalytic dialogue: Kleinian theory today. *J. Amer. Psychoanal. Assn*. 25: 363–70.

Sherfey, M. J. (1966). The evolution and nature of female sexuality in relation to psychoanalytic theory. *J. Amer. Psychoanal. Assn*. 14: 28–128.

Sklansky, M. (1972). Panel report: indications and contraindications for the psychoanalysis of the adolescent. *J. Amer. Psychoanal. Assn*. 20: 134–44.

Solnit, A. J. (1959). Panel report: the vicissitudes of ego development in adolescence. *J. Amer. Psychoanal. Assn*. 7: 523–36.

Spiegel, L. A. (1958). Comments on the psychoanalytic psychology of adolescence. *Psychoanal. Study Child* 13: 296–308.

Stewart, W. A. (1963). An inquiry into the concept of working through. *J. Amer. Psychoanal. Assn*. 11: 474–99.

Stoller, R. S. (1969). *Sex and Gender*. London: Hogarth Press.

Strachey, J. (1934). The nature of the therapeutic action of psychoanalysis. *Int. J. Psychoanal*. 15: 127–59.

Sugar, M. (1979). Therapeutic approaches to the borderline adolescent. *Adolescent Psychiatry* 7: 343–61.

Tanner, J. M. (1962). *Growth at Adolescence*. Oxford: Oxford Univ. Press.

Tausk, V. (1912). On masturbation. *Psychoanal. Study Child* 6(1951): 61–79.

———— (1919). On the origin of the "influencing machine" in schizophrenia. In *The Psychoanalytic Reader*, ed. R. Fliess. New York: Int. Univ. Press, 1948, pp. 31–64.

Tylim, I. (1978). Narcissistic transference and countertransference in adolescent treatment. *Psychoanal. Study Child* 33: 279–92.

Wexler, M. (1965). Working through in the therapy of schizophrenia. *Int. J. Psychoanal*. 46: 279–86.

Winnicott, D. W. (1953). Transitional objects and transitional phenomena: A study of the first not-me possession. *Int. J. Psychoanal*. 34: 89–97.

———— (1958). The capacity to be alone. *Int. J. Psychoanal*. 39: 416–20.

Index

Abortion: as rejected femininity, 62
Abraham, K., 31
Acting-out, 7
Adolescence: main developmental function of, 5, 21, 166, 181; central masturbation fantasy in, 6–10; normal and abnormal development, 9–10, 24–25; clinical material, 10–15; prolonged, 20; pregnancy and motherhood in, 61–62; end of, 187–89
Analyst: adolescent's use of transference relationship, 71–75; transference breakdown, 81–84; intervention in compulsive behavior, 136–38, 140–41; and adolescent's "sexual abnormality," 170–73. *See also* Transference
Anorexia nervosa, 102, 203
Anxiety: about body, 23, 53; masturbation conflict of female adolescents, 54–55; and assessment of psychopathology, 182
Assessment. *See* Developmental breakdown—assessment
Attempted suicide. *See* Suicide attempts
Autoerotic activity. *See* Masturbation

Bak, R. C., 109
Beres, D., 73
Bergman, A., 31, 66

Bernfeld, S., 20
Blos, P., 9, 20, 70, 110, 138, 166
Body: changes at puberty, 4–5, 40, 65; developmental breakdown as rejection of, 22–24; integration of, 29; relationship to, 36; ownership of, 38–39, 65, 166
Body image: vagina as part of, 25, 29, 32–35, 44–45, 193–94; functioning penis as part of, 25, 29, 193–94; idealized, 65–69
Borderline functioning; clinical material, 96–102
Breuer, J., 31
Brunswick, R. M., 53, 61

Castration: wish for and fear of, 12
Central masturbation fantasy. *See* Masturbation—central fantasy
Centre for Research into Adolescent Breakdown, 113n
Chasseguet-Smirgel, J., 163
Cohen, D. J., 66
Clower, V. L., 55
Compulsive behavior: intervention, to control, 136–38, 140–41, 156; central masturbation fantasy and, 138; and assessment of psychopathology, 182; anorexia nervosa, 203
Countertransference. *See* Transference

221

Hand: symbolic meaning of, 50–53, 54, 59–60
Harley, M., 10, 136, 169
Hoffer, W., 46, 51n
Homosexuality: in adolescence, 158–64; treatment issues, 162–64; assessment of, 165–169
Horney, K., 52

Idealized body image. *See* Body image
Incest barrier: and psychotic behavior or development, 23–24; and suicide attempts, 113–14. . *See also* Fantasies; Oedipus complex
Incestuous fantasies. *See* Fantasies
Intervention: dangerous compulsive behavior controlled by, 135–38, 140–41, 156. *See also* Analyst; Compulsive behavior

Jacobson, E., 31, 36, 68, 71, 110
Jones, E., 31, 52
Jung, C., 31

Katan, M., 111, 119, 156, 193
Kernberg, O. F., 31, 109
Klein, M., 31, 52, 109

Lampl-de Groot, J., 36, 169
Laufer, M., 70, 83
Lewin, B. C., 66
Limentani, A., 138, 167
Lindner, S., 50
Loewald, H. W., 28, 73, 81n, 166

Mahler, M. S., 6, 31, 66
Male-female differentiation: normal and abnormal development, 25–29; clinical material, 32–35, 162; rejection of, 168; establishment of, 187; sexual object's function in, 190
Masturbation: as trial action, 8–10, 26, 37–38; clinical material, 13,

17, 19, 33, 40–46; anxiety over, 37; Freud on, 37, 49–50; recurrent themes in, 46; male and female conflicts contrasted and compared, 49, 55; first phase of, 50–54; and idealized body image fantasy, 65–69
—central fantasy: discussion of, 6–10; in hierarchy of fantasies, 27; post-puberty, 29; clinical material, 33, 39–48, 88–94, 141, 156, 161–62; compulsive behavior and, 138
—female adolescent: Freud's view, 49, 52, 54; hand's symbolic meaning for, 51–53, 54, 59–60; conflict of, 54–56; clinical material, 56–59
Motherhood: in adolescence, 61–63

Narcissistic equilibrium: puberty's effect on, 65
Narcissistic personality disorder: clinical material, 102–11

Obers, S. J., 73
Object relationships, 7; and central masturbation fantasy, 7–8; and ego ideal, 69–71; assessment of psychopathology in, 181–82
Oedipus complex: resolution of, defined, 5, 6, 28–29; and developmental breakdown, 23n, 29–32; male-female differentiation, 25–29; Freud's view of, 29–31; female, 60–61
—preoedipal period: autoeroticism in, 6; Freud's views on, 31; central issue of, 53; body image fantasies of, 67
Ownership of the body. *See* Body

Pathology. *See* Psychopathology
Penis envy: Freud's view on, 49, 54; objections to theory of, 52

Perversion: Freud's use of term, 3; as sign of foreclosure of development, 163–64; "regressive" differentiated, 164
Phallic-oedipal period: male-female differentiation in, 28. *See also* Oedipus complex
Pine, F., 31, 66
Pregnancy, 61–62
Preoedipal child. *See* Oedipus complex
Primal-scene fantasies, 43–47. *See also* Fantasies
"Primary addiction," 39. *See also* Masturbation
Prolonged adolescence. *See* Adolescence
Promiscuity, 140
Pseudo ego ideal, 70
Psychoanalyst. *See* Analyst
Psychopathology: manifestations of, 21–22; "perverse" and "regressive," 164. *See also* Developmental breakdown
Psychotic episode, 7; suicide attempt as, 112–13; described, 195
Psychotic functioning: assessment of, 192–95; described, 195. *See also* Developmental breakdown—assessment
Psychotic process, ongoing: assessment of, 195
Puberty: changes occurring during, 4–5; post-puberty masturbation fantasies, 7; developmental breakdown at, 21–22, 27; effect on females, 54–55; narcissistic equilibrium affected by, 65

Reality: in suicide attempts, 144; perverse sexual activities in adolescence, 168; and assessment of psychopathology, 182
Reality testing, 23, 80, 168; body image linked to, 36

Reconstruction: primary function of, in adolescence, 84–86; clinical material, 146
Regression: in adolescence, 19; and transference, 72
Regressive pathology: "perverse" differentiated, 164
Repression: of superego, 65
Ritvo, S., 9, 55, 71, 73, 83, 110
Rosenfeld, H., 111, 138

Sandler, J., 73
Savior theme, 11
Schafer, R., 73
Schilder, P., 6, 119
Segal, H., 31
"Self-preservation instinct," 72
"Sexual abnormality": analyst's response to, 170–73
Sexual gratification: psychic and physical, 188
Sexual identity: defined, 5; suicide attempts and, 113; choice of procreation as central to establishment of, 188
Sexual intercourse: idealized body image fantasy, 68
Sexual maturity: adolescent reaction to, 23–24; genital integration in girls, 62–63
Sexual organization. *See* Final sexual organization
Sherfey, M. J., 52
Solnit, A. J., 73
Stewart, W. A., 120
Stoller, R. S., 167
Strachey, J., 156
Suicide attempts: clinical material, 15, 42–44, 101–02, 104–05, 109, 115, 122–31, 139–55; absence of guilt, 112, 115; as acute psychotic episode, 112, 120, 122; developmental breakdown, 113–14; signs of risk, 114–16, 204–07; depersonalization at time of, 116; thera-